"I have just read chapter 5 of  German shepherd, Charlie, an approval. That's my dog—lovi ing and quite literate. Congra sure-fire bestseller."

—Art Linkletter

"Amazing! This book is as terrific as the publisher says it is! Mort Crim, as always, delivers high value for time spent reading, listening or watching him. A rarity—thoughtful and humorous."

—Dan Rather
CBS News

"Here is an indication of how good this book is: I don't share Mort Crim's affection for dogs, but I *love* his book!"

—Rabbi Harold S. Kushner
author, *When Bad Things Happen to Good People*

"'A word aptly spoken is like apples of gold in settings of silver.' (Prov. 29:11)

"Mort Crim, from his wisdom and experience, has mined some beautiful nuggets of gold and set them in choice words of silver. This is a book to savor more than once."

—Pat Boone

"Mort Crim's years of experience in journalism pay off, once again, in this lovable, warm, touching book. If you aren't a dog lover now, you will be after you spend time with Mort through his *Second Thoughts*."

—Connie Chung
ABC News

"Mort's first-person account of how two dogs helped him through the trauma of losing his wife to cancer will move you from tears of grief to smiles of delight and eventually to howls of laughter. This book is not for dog lovers only—it's for anyone interested in living a richer, fuller life and a deeper understanding of what makes life terrific!"

—Dan Clark
author, *Puppies for Sale* and *Simon Says*

Second Thoughts On:

How to *Be* as Terrific as Your Dog Thinks You *Are!*

Mort Crim

Health Communications, Inc.
Deerfield Beach, Florida

www.hci-online.com
www.mortcrim.com

Library of Congress Cataloging-in-Publication Data

Crim, Mort.
    Second thoughts on : how to be as terrific as your dog
thinks you are / Mort Crim.
        p.   cm.
    ISBN 1-55874-784-2 (trade paper)
    1. Conduct of life.   2. Dogs—Psychological aspects.
I. Title: How to be as terrific as your dog thinks you are.
II. Title.
BF637.C5 C76 2000
158—dc21
                                                00-025331

Publisher: Health Communications, Inc.
            3201 S.W. 15th Street
            Deerfield Beach, Florida 33442-8190

Cover design by Lisa Camp
Book inside design by Anthony Clausi
Cover photo of Doberman by Albert Crim
Cover photo of dachshund by Carey Crim
Cover photos of Mort Crim courtesy of Mort Crim
    Communications, Inc.

This book is dedicated with love,
gratitude and warm memories to

Golum

a gentle Doberman who would be embarrassed
by such an honor,

and

Bogey

a lovable but cocky little dachshund who
would figure *he* deserved it!

Special thanks to all the other pets whose lives have touched ours over the years, many of whom provided material for this book. They include: Zoey, Ouija, Ginger, Jinx, Susie, JoJo, Teddy, Taffy, Chenne Brun, Bear, Erika, Scruffy, Smokey, Jamie, Rusty, Porky, Spotty, Rags, Irene, Sarge, Scruffy, Twiggy, Buffy, Fluffy Agamemnon, Axel, Sierra Sara Mack, Tinka, Malcolm and Chester.

Also by Mort Crim

Like It Is

One Moment, Please

Second Thoughts: One Hundred Upbeat Messages for Beat-Up Americans

Good News for a Change

Contents

Introduction

*Whoever said you can't buy happiness
forgot about puppies.*

—Gene Hill

Hello. My name is Mort, and I'm a recovering dog lover.

I know this addiction can never be cured but at the moment mine *is* under control.

Understand, this *condition* does not make me a bad person. Medical science is beginning to recognize that loving dogs is not a sign of moral weakness nor, necessarily, a character defect.

Heredity may be a factor: Some people seem genetically predisposed to handle their love of dogs better than others.

Clearly some of us can't handle it at all.

We are the ones whose pulses quicken at the sight of a golden retriever plunging into the lake to fetch a stick.

Who can't pass a pet store window where beagle pups are playing without wanting one—or half a dozen.

Who can't see a photograph of an abandoned cocker spaniel in the newspaper without wishing to adopt every dog at the local pound.

There is some comfort in knowing we don't suffer alone. Americans and Canadians are probably the most dog-crazy people in the world. Four-fifths of us who own any kind of pet own dogs.

More than half say that if they were marooned on an island they'd prefer having their dog with them rather than another human.

A third of us dog owners call our dogs on the phone when we're out of town. And two-thirds of us take them with us on vacation.

Only those of us who've hit rock bottom fully understand the impact—and the cost— of loving dogs: the chewed furniture, stained carpets, nights of barking, days of *barfing*, angry neighbors, pooper-scoopers, threatened lawsuits, vet bills and boarding charges.

Like all addicts, dog lovers can't be helped until they admit they have a problem. Such insight occurs at different times, in different ways.

For me, the moment of truth came one night as I attempted to sneak Golum into a motel that did not permit pets. Since Golum was a Doberman, this was not easy. It required both strategy and subterfuge.

As I opened a rear door plainly marked *Emergency Exit Only,* a loud alarm went off. A desk clerk and a security guard rushed toward me but stopped halfway down the hall as Golum stiffened his stance and assumed the "I-think-you-may-want-to-reconsider-this" pose.

Wisely choosing to avoid direct confrontation, the desk clerk coolly invited us to seek some other motel—immediately. As we drove out of the parking lot, I understood for the first time just how much my *habit* had changed me.

I could deal with the bills, the barking and the blotched carpets. But how could I live with the knowledge that loving a dog had reduced me to the level of a common sneak?

Recovery was not immediate. Golum remained a faithful and loving companion until his death. But an increasingly demanding travel schedule—and the arrival of a spoiled-rotten cat—helped me gain some control over my canine-caring impulses.

So far, we have not acquired another dog. But the temptation is strong, and I recognize that it will always be there. Since there is no cure, the best I can do is try to guard against any moment of weakness.

When photos of homeless puppies show up in our paper, I quickly turn to the sports pages.

When we pass a pet store, I stare at the goldfish.

The hardest part is when I see someone playing with a dog. Romping through the woods. Strolling along the lake. Tossing a stick or a Frisbee.

All I can do in such circumstances is try very hard not to think about Golum—the walks we took, the sorrows we shared, the fun we had.

But, of course, I do think about him a lot. I can't look at another dog without remembering how loyal Golum was. How brave and strong; yet kind and loving. I think often about his wild enthusiasm for life.

Best of all, I remember this:

Golum thought I was *terrific*!

One

A Friend in Need

A dog is the only thing on Earth that loves
you more than he loves himself.
—Josh Billings

Within eight months I had become both a widower and an empty-nester.

In January, 1989, cancer claimed my wife of thirty-four years.

The following August, our daughter left for college. Our other child, a son, had left years earlier and now was in graduate school.

The two-story house that had seemed just the right size as our kids were growing up suddenly was much too large. A man and two dogs could easily get lost in it.

It wasn't just the expanse of the house that no longer felt right: What had been a warm, inviting place now felt cold. The fireplace didn't seem to put out as much heat. The

table lamps weren't as bright. A dreariness—
a darkness—had settled over the house. The
silence was deafening.

When Nicki was alive, the *house* was alive.
It had been both love nest and battleground.
Sanctuary and school. Refuge and retreat.
Library and hospital.

A place to rear children, nurture dreams,
climb up ladders, fall off diets, cook outside,
entertain, nurse a bad cold or tend to a
scraped knee.

It was a place to talk, watch TV, read a book,
laugh, cry, play, pray, work, rest and celebrate
holidays. Our house was where Nicki and I
could escape from the world or where we
could find renewed energy to take it on.

Now she was gone. Our dreams had been
dashed. The music had stopped. The light
was out. Silence replaced laughter. Ghosts of
a happier past lurked in every room. Why not
just move? After all, it was only Golum, Bogey
and me against the world. And in this tomb-
like house that used to be a *home*, the world
seemed to be winning.

But friends told me what I already knew:
Moving is one of life's major traumas, and I'd
had enough trauma for one year.

So that house, with its superfluous space and bittersweet memories, would just have to do—at least for awhile. The three of us would tough it out.

Life was lonely. Anyone who's ever lost a spouse either to death or divorce knows that nights can be the worst.

As a television news anchor in Detroit, I typically arrived home after midnight. The stillness that waited for me there was mercifully broken by the inevitable sounds of joy coming from my two buddies—Golum and Bogey.

After an evening in the newsroom, surrounded by friends and colleagues—an environment alive with energy, action and *life*— that empty house might have been unbearable without those two eager friends.

Walking through that door each night meant reentering a private world of silence and grief, a world where memories were too painful to provide the solace they later would bring.

Golum and Bogey brought comfort *now*. In the depths of despair, I began forging a new relationship with my dogs. The irony is they weren't *my* dogs. When Al and Carey went away to college, Golum and Bogey were among the possessions they left behind—along with theater costumes and hockey sticks.

Christopher Montgomery Bogart joined our family when Carey was eight. He was her Christmas present that year.

Al's dog, Golum, came to us some time later, after Al was in college, and *his* arrival was a surprise. As a pup, Golum had been abandoned along a highway and ended up in the dog pound, destined for either adoption or execution.

A college friend of Al's initially took Golum, but the pit bull he already owned wasn't too

Golum and my son, Al

Bogey

pleased about having competition. Recognizing that a return to the pound would mean almost certain death for the young Doberman, Al volunteered to take him. After all, Mom and Dad already were foster grandparents to his and Carey's two dogs still living at home. Why would they object to keeping a third until time for Al's return to college? Besides, knowing their weakness for dogs, all he had to do was show up with Golum, right? It was a brilliant strategy. And, it worked.

Bogey was a miniature dachshund; Golum, a red Doberman. Jinx, Al's older dog, was a mixed-breed mutt who seemed to be more dalmatian than anything else.

Jinx and Al

At seventy pounds, Golum was bigger than the other two combined. However, Bogey, smallest of the group, had seniority and this runt of a wiener dog wasn't about to surrender tenure to an upstart—even one five times his size.

It was clear Bogey had never looked in a mirror and never recognized how small he was.

So even though Golum was biggest and strongest, Bogey quickly established himself as top dog at our house. Golum's bark could strike terror into the heart of any mail carrier, but he would always stand aside and allow Bogey to walk through a door first!

If Golum got to the back-porch chaise ahead of Bogey, Bogey would stare at him and within a few seconds, Golum would be thoroughly intimidated.

Bogey, Jinx and my daughter, Carey

He would then nervously slink off the chaise allowing Bogey to jump up, triumphantly, and take over the spot he believed Golum had been warming—just for him.

Technically, Golum and Bogey would always belong to Al and Carey. But when kids go off to school, technicalities are irrelevant. Possession, after all, does count for nine points.

Jinx was old by the time Golum arrived, and she died not long afterward. But Golum and Bogey remained at home when Carey left for college and Al returned to his graduate studies. As a practical matter, these two dogs were now mine, for better or for worse.

It turned out for the better.

Two

Terrific Is as Terrific Does

To his dog, every man is Napoleon.
—Aldous Huxley

Don't accept your dog's admiration as conclusive evidence that you are wonderful.
—Ann Landers

Let's face it: A main reason we love dogs is because they love us. Unabashedly. Unashamedly. Unreservedly.

It has nothing to do with our worth. Our bank account. Our looks. Or even our attitude. Dogs love us because it's their nature to love, unconditionally.

People rarely are like that. During my years in television, viewers responded positively to me if I said something on the air they considered witty or funny or profound or in any other way worthy. If I said something stupid or corny or offensive or—heaven forbid—inaccurate, they vented their displeasure with calls or letters.

Clearly, any *love* my fans felt for me was conditional. It was predicated upon performance. It had much to do with what I *did* and little to do with who I *was*.

With Golum and Bogey, it was different. Once I walked into the house, it didn't matter to them if I'd embarrassed myself and the family name with some bonehead remark only an hour earlier.

They jumped and barked and greeted me with unbounded enthusiasm. It was reassuring to know that somewhere within my viewing audience were at least two creatures who would accept, forgive, adore and be loyal to me no matter what! In a word, these guys flat-out thought I was terrific.

Of course, I knew better. I knew the rest of the audience knew better. If only these dogs knew the real me with all my flaws and weaknesses—if they knew as much about my failings as the viewers knew—surely they wouldn't believe I was all that great. Or would they?

Acceptance seems so natural to dogs. Perhaps even if they were capable of understanding how badly I blundered sometimes, how selfishly I could behave, how incompetent I could be—perhaps even then they'd still think I was terrific. Maybe their attitude had more to do with them than with me.

Then I started thinking: What if I *could* measure up to their high regard? Become all the things they seem to think I am? What could I do to merit their admiration? How could I become terrific—as terrific as my dogs think I am?

Suddenly it hit me. I would simply need to be more like my dogs. The qualities that would deserve their devotion are precisely the qualities they have: enthusiasm, loyalty, bravery, acceptance, forgiveness. If I could just develop the characteristics they seem to think I possess, I'd be entitled to their esteem.

Here I was, living every day with two of the finest role models anyone could ever hope to emulate.

Already they had attained levels of success in life I could only aspire to—such as the ability to start their day without caffeine.

The capacity to remain cheerful despite any aches and pains.

To eat the same food every day and be grateful for it.

To take criticism without carrying a grudge.

To live in peaceful harmony with each other

despite the fact they weren't the same color.

These guys even knew how to have a great time without booze.

And they were so honest, they were willing to *do their business* in public!

That's it. If I wanted to be as terrific as my dogs thought I was, I would have to become more like my dogs.

Three

Even Short Tails Can Wag

The worst bankrupt in the world is the man who has lost his enthusiasm.
—H. W. Arnold

No animal should ever jump up on the dining room furniture unless absolutely certain that he can hold his own in the conversation.
—Fran Lebowitz

Golum and Bogey never had a bad day.

Bad moments, yes—as when scolded for misbehaving, or getting a shot from the vet. But as soon as the unpleasantness was over, their old vim and vigor quickly returned.

When some event didn't suit them, these two simply dealt with it and moved on. They never moped or pouted. Even as age and arthritis began taking a toll in their later years, these happy dogs refused to let stiffness and pain rob them of their zest.

Golum and Bogey loved life—and lived life —enthusiastically. Theirs was a joy that came from their hearts. But it manifested itself most dramatically in their butts.

At the slightest hint of fun—the rattle of a leash, the opening of food—both dogs immediately went into a tailspin.

Bogey, who still *had* a tail, would start a rapid back and forth motion like a windshield wiper. But Golum, whose tail had been bobbed in keeping with good Doberman grooming standards, merely rotated his.

However, as his excitement grew, he would twirl that stub so fast it appeared his hindquarters might, at any moment, become airborne. Golum didn't have as much appendage as Bogey had, but what he had he used with ebullience. Even a short tail can wag impressively when linked to a soul full of delight.

Their enthusiasm was contagious, and enthusiasm was something I badly needed to *catch* during those dreary and difficult months following Nicki's death. How could any creature be so happy? What was the secret of their great gusto? Surely, to be as terrific as they thought I was, I would need to rediscover the excitement I'd lost.

I fully understood that this would take time. Grief has its own calendar. But I also knew

Golum and Bogey were on my side. I knew they would lead the way.

For dogs, enthusiasm seems to be built in. They don't have to think about it or work at it. Enthusiasm comes as part of the canine package—as standard as barking and sleeping.

We humans, on the other hand, don't always find it so natural. After several years of wrestling with life, of encountering defeats and disappointments, of suffering losses, we may find our supply of enthusiasm so depleted we forget whether we ever had any.

Watching Golum and Bogey romp in our backyard one sunny, spring afternoon, I knew that, in time, I, too, would feel like playing again.

Nicki and I had shared an optimistic view of life. She had made it clear she didn't want that part of our marriage partnership to die with her.

"Honey, please don't grieve too long," she had said to me only a few days before her death. "I want you to build a new life. It's really important that you move on with your life."

The excruciating pain I felt in that moment made it difficult for me to really hear what she was saying. But now, watching those dogs frisking about among the early spring flowers, gave Nicki's admonition fresh meaning. What she had wanted for me was exactly what I would have wanted for her had I been the one to leave first.

What she had urged was that I never lose my enthusiasm for life. That I never allow tragedy or sadness to have the last word.

Faith in God, belief in the meaning and the goodness of life, were at the heart of her philosophy and had been since we'd met as childhood sweethearts. So I readily understood the full scope of what she was communicating with those few simple words, "I want you to build a new life."

There was no doubt in my mind that, in due course, I would rediscover a reason to live, that enthusiasm would be rekindled and hope renewed. What Nicki and I believed—what we had shared—transcended our physical presence together.

I had seen my mother rediscover joy after losing the most important person in her life —my father. They'd loved each other deeply and exclusively for forty-four years, and we wondered how she would survive such a devastating loss. But Dad, like Nicki, had left a heritage of hope. Of faith. Of enthusiasm for life. A conviction that we were all created for a purpose and that death is not a dead end but a passage. Because Dad never lost his belief in the meaning, the goodness and the ultimate triumph of life, my mother was able to rebuild hers.

When Dad was dean of students at a small southern college, he once counseled a sophomore named Harold. One of Harold's professors had told Dad that the young man had ability but lacked enthusiasm. He was apathetic.

Harold appeared emotionless as he walked into Dad's office. He sat slouched in a chair as Dad tried to draw him out of his indifference and engage him in conversation. Harold responded to Dad with a blank stare.

"Harold," Dad said, "Your professor tells me you're apathetic." Still nothing.

"Harold, do you understand the word *apathetic*?"

Finally Harold responded, "No, and I couldn't care less."

Apathy is a crime against existence itself,

and it's one we shouldn't tolerate indefinitely in ourselves.

Sure, life will deal cruel blows to all of us. There will be sadness. Failures. Disappointments. Keeping the flame of enthusiasm flickering at such times isn't easy. But it is essential. And it is possible.

How do we do it? For one thing, we have to allow healing to occur. When Bogey was about two years old, he cut his leg, and the gash was deep enough that we took him to the vet.

As the doctor finished taping on a bandage, he said, "The wound should heal within a week if you can keep him from chewing off the bandage and getting to his stitches."

That's the secret. How many of our wounds would heal if we'd only allow them to? Emotional wounds. Psychological hurts.

But like our little dog, we're instinctively driven to revisit the wound. To keep examining it. Ultimately, that slows the healing process and delays a return of enthusiasm.

I once visited an elderly relative whose husband had died five years earlier. She had left everything in his bedroom exactly as it was the day he died. The belt that he'd placed on a dresser was there, untouched, as were several other personal items.

The woman had turned the bedroom into a shrine. She had refused to let go of her pain, so her grief was as sharp as it had been five years earlier.

When their son was four, Rabbi Harold Kushner and his wife learned that the child had progeria—the disease that causes rapid aging. This meant the boy would lose all his hair and look like an old man before he reached puberty.

At age fourteen, their son died.

It's difficult to imagine any greater grief than that which accompanies the loss of a child. But from that bitter experience, Rabbi Kushner was able later to write, "Pain does not last forever." Yes, pain will subside. Enthusiasm will reemerge if we allow it to happen.

In the final analysis, enthusiasm isn't a function of fate.

It's often an issue of time, but it's always a matter of choice:

When the U.S. Navy first launched its Polaris submarines, it was decided that each sub should have two complete crews. Each crew would alternate so that each got six months at sea, six months ashore.

When one of the veteran crewmen was asked how he liked the system, he replied, enthusiastically, "It's great. Whether you get along with your wife or whether you don't, you get six months of happiness every year."

That crewman had *decided* this arrangement would be a win-win no matter what.

If you seem a little short on enthusiasm today, try using what you've got. See how it multiplies.

You'll discover that even short tails can wag.

Four

It Will Be Different This Time

Gladness of the heart is the life of a man,
and the joyfulness of a man prolongeth
his days.
—Ecclesiasticus 30:22

The last of the human freedoms—to choose
one's attitude in any given set of
circumstances.
—Viktor Frankl

L et's go for a ride," I yelled from the kitchen.

Within seconds, Golum bounded in from the den, eyes sparkling, tail-stub wagging, his entire body performing the sort of excited dance he always executed when something terrific was about to happen.

As I snapped the leash onto his collar, Golum's anticipation exploded into more feverish animation. He could hardly contain himself. This was going to be a wonderful adventure. This would be the mother of all car rides.

What's amazing about this is that Golum was expecting the *best*. Why? How could he?

Had he totally forgotten that the last ten times we'd put him in the car, he'd gone to the kennel?

And he distinctly disliked the kennel. Why did he think this time would be different?

The answer was clear: Golum was the *eternal optimist*.

Golum

No matter how many previous car rides had ended in disappointment, *this* ride—he was convinced—would end in success.

If we want to be as terrific as our dogs think we are, then we'll need to acquire their optimism. Like them, we'll have to shake off disappointments of the past so that they don't contaminate our hopes for the future.

Most of us begin life with huge reservoirs of optimism. As children, we expect to win every game we play. We expect our parents to love us, the tooth fairy to leave money under our pillow, Santa to bring us great gifts and summer vacations to be absolutely wonderful. As children, life is our oyster, and it's filled with pearls. No pooch in the neighborhood is more upbeat about life than we are when we're very young.

Then, life begins to happen. Negative experiences start to drain off some of this exuberance. We discover that we don't win every game. We don't ace every test. We don't get everything we want for Christmas. We miss a long-anticipated picnic because we're sick.

As we become adults, even tougher challenges siphon off our optimism. Our number-one college choice doesn't accept us. The job we'd set our hearts on fails to materialize. A grandparent—or a parent—dies. A love interest rejects us. We begin to realize that life is hard. It's filled with disappointments. There are no guarantees.

In time, that deep reservoir of hope and optimism we began with not only has been drained, it may have been replaced by a most noxious substance: cynicism.

A pessimist will tell you that cynicism is the only *practical* way to approach life. After all, isn't a pessimist only a realist who once trusted an optimist? So the pessimist's motto becomes, "Expect nothing in life and you'll never be disappointed."

The problem is, pessimism doesn't work. Both history and common sense support the notion that optimism is the only practical philosophy. Why? First, because only optimists accomplish anything worthwhile. Second, because only optimists find it worthwhile to accomplish anything.

If you don't believe that it's optimists who move the world forward, consider this: How many stamps have been issued, how many coins minted, how many statues erected to honor the life and work of a pessimist?

Most of the world's great leaders—in science, medicine, industry, education, religion, government—have been individuals who believed, deeply, that they could make a difference. And, they believed that making a difference mattered.

Pessimists, on the other hand, are under no such illusions. Life stinks. The problems are intractable and unsolvable. Besides, nobody cares, so why should they? It's a dog-eat-dog world.

The best they can hope for is to accumulate whatever they can for their own benefit and to hell with everybody else.

They approach life's challenges with a gloominess satirically expressed by Woody Allen:

> More than any time in history mankind faces a crossroads. One path leads to despair and utter hopelessness, the other to total extinction. Let us pray that we have the wisdom to choose correctly.

The person who wakes up in the morning expecting the worst is unlikely to perform admirably. That's why, no matter how short our own reserves of optimism, we instinctively seek out optimistic people to work for us. Would you engage a surgeon to operate on you who doubted the operation would be a success? Would you step aboard an airline piloted by a captain who didn't believe he or she could complete the flight safely?

The story of how Thomas Edison invented the light bulb has become legendary.

When a friend pointed out that Edison had failed in nearly a hundred attempts before finally figuring out how to do it, Edison corrected him. Those weren't failures, the great inventor explained. He had merely discovered about a hundred ways *not* to make a light bulb.

Had Edison lost his optimism and become cynical on the eightieth or ninetieth attempt, it would have fallen to someone else—someone more hopeful—to create this device that changed history.

But there's another story about Edison, not quite as well known, which illustrates the extent of the man's optimistic nature. It was told by his son, Charles, who recalled the 1914 fire that nearly destroyed Edison's laboratories in West Orange, New Jersey.

Edison lost nearly two million dollars worth of equipment and records documenting much of his life's work. Charles wrote of seeing his dad standing near the fire, his face ruddy in the glow, his white hair blown by winter winds.

Charles Edison said, "My heart ached for

him. He was no longer young. And everything was being destroyed." But the next morning, as he walked along the charred embers of so many hopes and dreams, Thomas Edison, then sixty-seven years old, said:

> There is great value in disaster. All our mistakes arc burned up. Thank God we can start anew.

Clearly, most of us would like to be optimistic. We'd like to be hopeful about life. But where do we *find* the confidence that things will get better? How do we refill those depleted reservoirs with the real thing? After all, we don't want to trick ourselves. Become Pollyannas. Bury our heads in the sand.

It's a question we all must answer for ourselves. But there are some qualities most optimistic people I've met and interviewed have in common.

First, they're giving, unselfish people who believe it's important to help others.

Second, they possess a deep faith that life has meaning, that they were *created* for a purpose—that existence is much more than some cosmic accident.

Both of these concepts were ingrained in me at a very young age. Both formed the foundation for my optimism. It is to these beliefs that I turn today whenever my reservoir is low.

Born into a family of ministers, missionaries and teachers, I learned early, by both word and example, that *service to others* is the highest calling. I was taught that such service is an *attitude*, not a profession; no matter what job we hold, our real vocation is to serve.

Whether in the classroom, the pulpit, the business office, the hospital, the TV studio, on the construction project or the assembly line, we were all put here to help others.

Furthermore, it matters greatly that we do so.

A small sign hung on my grandmother's living room wall. I remember seeing it before I was old enough to read. She would read the sign to me and, therefore, it contained some of the first words I would learn. The sign's words were taken from the Bible and it said:

All things work together for good to those who love God.

What a marvelous heritage of optimism those few but profound words provided. They were a simple statement of my family's faith —that if we did our part, if we lived up to our responsibilities, we didn't have to worry about outcomes. In the final analysis, on the great cosmic scale of justice, it would all come out okay.

Because my grandparents—and parents— believed that true love of God meant love for each other, their message to me was clear: Live a life of caring and of service, make your contribution, give it your best, and you won't have to lie awake at night worrying about consequences.

In the words of Stonewall Jackson, "Do your best and leave the rest to Providence." Jackson wasn't one to fret over possible outcomes. Optimism propelled him through all of life's difficulties.

It was an attitude Golum certainly would have understood.

If we want to be as terrific as our dogs think we are, we must approach each day, each obstacle with the firm conviction that "It will be different, this time."

Five

A Dog Is a Dog

I wonder if other dogs think poodles are
members of a weird religious cult?
—Rita Rudner

Prejudice is the reason of fools.
—Voltaire

Golum was color-blind.

I have no medical evidence to support this assertion. It was never confirmed by a veterinarian. It's just something I observed.

Golum never seemed to recognize that he was brown and Bogey was black. If he did, it certainly didn't matter to him.

For a short time, Golum and Bogey shared our home with Al's first pet, an older dog named Jinx. She was of dubious heritage, and the only *papers* she ever had were the ones used to train her. However, Jinx was a good old girl, not terribly bright, but wonderfully gentle and loving.

Did I mention Jinx was white? That didn't seem to bother either Golum *or* Bogey. And it didn't make any difference to Jinx that the other two dogs were "of color." Apparently, all three dogs were color-blind. Consequently, they lived together, ate together, played together, slept together and generally had a great time.

Jinx and Bogey

If you and I ever hope to be as terrific as our dogs think we are, we'll have to become color-blind. Because it's impossible to be prejudiced and terrific at the same time.

Not only is bigotry morally reprehensible, it's impractical. Consider the lost lives and wasted resources that have resulted from ethnic and religious conflict in the Balkans. In Africa. In the Middle East. In Northern Ireland. *In the United States.*

Religious and racial hatred know no national boundaries. They exist in the human heart and infect people of all ages at all levels of society. The wealthy and the poor. The educated and the ignorant. No one is immune to the devastating virus of bigotry.

A branch librarian thought things looked different when she came to work one morning. She was right. A young intern the night before had rearranged all the books according to color. Isn't that a stupid way to categorize books? Or people?

Some categorizing in life makes sense. But classifying people by the color of their skin, the place of their birth or the method they choose to worship makes no sense at all.

In my workshop, I have some sorting bins.

Wood screws are separated out from metal screws, then further organized by size and whether they have a slot head or a Phillip's head.

This *sorting* serves a logical purpose. It saves lots of time when I'm looking for precisely the right size and type screw for a particular job.

A lot of categorizing makes sense, and sometimes we identify the categories in visible ways: Uniforms worn on duty make it clear who is a police officer, an airline captain, a football player, a surgeon or a chef. Such categories make life simpler both for those being "categorized" and for those of us interested in their services.

But religious, racial and ethnic categorizing make no sense at all. To brand people as good or bad, worthy or unworthy, smart or stupid, based upon such criteria is idiotic.

When we try to *sort out people* based upon their philosophy, their accent or their skin pigmentation, we're placing them in little boxes, neat, tidy—and wrong. We're treating human beings as though they were as simple and uncomplicated as parts scattered on a workbench.

Such categorizing ignores the intrinsic worth of all people and the unique talents and capabilities they possess as individuals.

Jane Kermani, a homemaker in Davenport, Iowa, wanted to make certain her little boys never fell into the deplorable and dangerous trap of bigotry.

When her two sons began noticing—and commenting upon the fact—that people come in different shapes, sizes and colors, Jane placed several eggs on the counter.

She pointed out that some eggs were white, some brown, some were large and some small. Then, she cracked all the eggs, put them into a bowl and asked her sons if they could tell which was which.

Of course, they couldn't. All the yolks looked the same.

If only we could all grasp that simple lesson: Whatever our outside shell, inside we're all pretty much alike. Golum, Bogey and Jinx understood, and their lives were richer and healthier for it.

Not only were our dogs oblivious to *color*, they also weren't impressed by *credentials*. Bogey was the only one of the three who had bona fide registration papers. Those papers showed his legal name as Christopher Montgomery Bogart, but he much preferred the more common nickname, Bogey.

Never did he park himself in a corner and refuse to respond until someone recognized the superiority of his heritage.

(Of course, anyone who's ever owned a dachshund knows it isn't necessary to build self-esteem in these little guys. They come with it built in.)

My mother's dog, Teddy, not only had a pedigree, he had a *college* degree. Teddy, a Shih Tzu who could trace his lineage back to Chinese royalty, had been to obedience school, or, as Mother preferred to call it, *Doggie University*. His diploma barely was big enough to contain his full, legal name, Ocie's Teddy Bear Tsing. You can understand why he was called *Teddy*.

When Teddy came to visit, our home had all the makings of a major one-upsmanship contest. Golum was biggest. Jinx was dumbest. Bogey was longest. Teddy was the best educated. They all came from different backgrounds, were of different colors and possessed different temperaments. Amazingly, none of those differences ever *made* a difference.

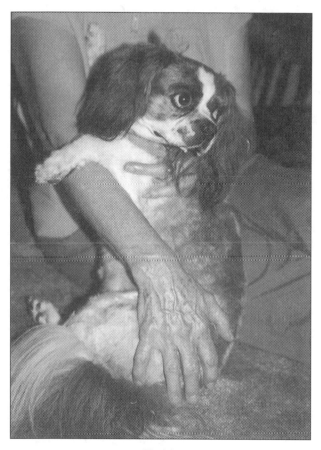

Teddy

Watching them play in the house or the yard, it was apparent that a dog is a dog. And if we ever want to *be* as terrific as they think we *are*, then we have to ignore differences the way they do.

Prejudice, of course, isn't always about race, religion or social standing. Bias can result from all kinds of differences:

My good friend, Dan Clark, has written a most touching story, set in a pet shop—a story so compelling that it was made into a short movie with Jack Lemmon playing the store owner.

A child entered the shop to buy a puppy and asked the owner how much it would cost. The man told him his puppies cost anywhere from thirty to fifty dollars.

Reaching into his pocket, the boy pulled out $2.37 and said, "Can I please look at them?"

The store owner smiled and whistled and out of the kennel came Lady, followed by five tiny balls of fur. One little puppy had a bad limp and when the store owner explained that the puppy would be permanently crippled, the boy said, "He's the one I want to buy."

The pet shop owner said, "No, you don't want to buy this puppy. I'll just give him to you. He's never going to be able to run and jump and play with you like the other puppies."

The child protested. "No, sir. That puppy's just as good as any of the others, and I'll give you something every week until he's paid for."

Then the boy reached down, rolled up his

pant leg to reveal a badly twisted, crippled left leg, supported by a big, metal brace.

He looked up at the store owner and said, softly:

"I don't run so well myself, and the little puppy will need someone who understands."

There is an honesty, a humility about dogs that refuses to recognize those artificial categories we humans construct so we can make sure everybody is in the *right box*. What matters most to a dog is not *who* you are but *what* you are.

A rather arrogant university professor, whose research work had brought him world renown and numerous international honors, was trying to push his way to the head of the line at an airport ticket counter. He shouted at the agent, "I have to be on this flight and it has to be first class."

The agent kept assuring the pushy passenger that she'd get to him just as soon as she'd taken care of the people ahead of him. Finally, the impatient professor bullied his way to the counter, slapped his ticket down in front of the agent, and bellowed, "Lady, do you have any idea who I am?"

The woman smiled politely, then picked up

her public address microphone and announced for the entire terminal to hear: "Ladies and gentlemen, we have a passenger here who doesn't seem to know who he is. If anyone can help him find his identity, please come to the gate."

The assertive passenger retreated passively to the end of the line as the other waiting passengers broke into applause.

Arrogance is just another word for bigotry. To think we're better than someone else simply because we may have more money, more education, more prominence or better social skills is to reveal a serious deficiency in our own character. The greatest people in the world never have to be told how great they are.

Some of the smartest people I've ever known never had the benefit of a formal education. Some of the richest people weren't wealthy, but they were rich in friendships, purpose and a healthy sense of self. Some of the most wonderful people I've ever known seriously lacked social graces, but they were a joy to be around because they were *real*. And they were honest. Not like the character in this verse:

He lost his dough, he lost his job,
And yet, throughout his life,
He took his troubles like a *man*,
He blamed them on his *wife*!

I never remember any of our dogs trying to blame another when they messed up. If a carpet was stained, a chair chewed or a shoe missing, the offending pet inevitably showed signs of unmistakable guilt. The head would bow. Eyes drooped. Usually the culpable one would slink slowly to the floor, preparing for the stern lecture to come. Occasionally there would be clear signs of remorse but *never* any attempt to shift responsibility.

The relationship dogs have with each other isn't always smooth, but it is honest. They may occasionally growl at each other—even fight—but never over something so silly as color, training or pedigree.

To a dog, another dog is just a dog. Not a white dog. Not a black dog. Not an educated dog. Not a purebred dog. Just a dog.

And we have the nerve to call *them* dumb animals!

Six

Enter the Cat Lady

In order to keep a true perspective of
one's importance, everyone should have
a dog that will worship him and a cat
that will ignore him.

—Dereke Bruce

If you've ever heard two cats fighting, you know the kind of screeching, yowling, hissing and howling such a conflict can produce. But such a skirmish is an absolute *love-in* compared to the battles humans sometimes wage over which is superior—cats or dogs!

Having read thus far, you know that this author is a confirmed, born-and-bred, dyed-in-the-wool, give-no-ground, take-no-prisoners *dog* person. From my first cocker spaniel to my last Doberman pinscher, I'm canine through and through.

All my life I'd looked at cats the way my University of Michigan friends look at Ohio

State Buckeyes—with barely disguised contempt. What good is a cat, anyway?

They almost never come when called, hate to go swimming with you, refuse to fetch sticks, climb onto your lap only if they feel like it, and generally display a haughty independence that's anathema to any self-respecting dog lover.

Dogs, on the other hand, are *needy* creatures. Cats don't need anybody, so who needs them? Besides, what do they do? They're hardly equipped for anything except sitting— or lying—around the house waiting for everyone to proclaim how wonderful they are.

The difference between a cat and a dog is crystal clear: A dog considers how well his master cares for him and thinks, "Wow, *he* must be terrific."

A cat considers how well her master cares for her and thinks, "Wow, *I* must be terrific."

Cats never work. Did you ever hear of a Seeing Eye Siamese? A search and rescue Persian? Can you imagine going bird hunting with a Himalayan? How many cats would it take to pull a sled in Alaska? Let a policeman unleash his tabby on a fleeing criminal, and the crook might fall over and laugh himself to death.

Well, throughout my life that was pretty much my not-so-objective opinion of cats. Not that I disliked them, particularly. I've always had a soft spot for *all* animals.

As a child, I adopted my share of mice, hamsters—even snakes. But owning a cat? That was something I didn't really need to do . . . in this lifetime.

Enter the *cat lady!*

It's a funny thing about second marriages. You don't just get a new wife: You acquire the entire package. Children. In-laws. Furniture. Stored boxes. History. Political preferences. Pet preferences. They all come down the aisle with that new bride.

What I got with Alice Irene Miller was a *wonderful* package. Two handsome, intelligent and thoughtful sons, warm and accepting in-laws and some excellent antique furniture.

Her boxes? Well, I already had so many stored in the attic that hers would have plenty of company. History? We shared much. Our fathers both had been ministers in the same denomination. We shared college connections and many friends we'd both known over the years.

Well, there was the matter of politics and pets. But Irene (I call her Renee) was so thoughtful, so intelligent, so sensitive and compassionate, I knew that in time, I could bring her around to see things my way on these two subjects.

How we voted was, after all, a rather private matter. It wasn't something we ever *had* to settle. The *cat* issue was something else.

But since it was only a theoretical difference—i.e., we didn't *have* a cat—it seemed like an area best left unexamined. With so much in common, with so many things that we *liked* about each other, why let politics or pets mess up a good thing?

Renee clearly understood my devotion to dogs. Immediately after our first date, I'd driven her from the restaurant to my home to meet Golum and Bogey. (It was much later that I took her to meet my children and my mother.) So Renee could have had no illusions about my preference in pets.

Nor was she bashful about stating hers. Almost from the beginning Renee was engaged in a subtle but unmistakable propaganda campaign aimed at indoctrinating me about the value and the virtues of cats. It was never a full attack such as dinner conversation. It was always small skirmishes:

A glowing comment when she'd see a cat in the newspaper. A downright *gooey* response whenever she'd encounter a neighbor's real, live kitty. Every cat she met was sweet. Cute. Adorable. The fact that Renee always referred to even the oldest, ugliest, fattest cat as a *kitty* must have been part of her campaign to soften me up.

Men can be slow when it comes to clues. So despite weeks of subliminal suggestion and some brazen brainwashing, I was not quite prepared for what happened on that warm July night.

Our house had a pool, and it was part of our routine to take a swim after I arrived home from delivering the late TV newscast. This particular night, Renee called to me from the patio, "Mort, as soon as you've changed into your bathing suit, I have a surprise for you."

Shock would have been a better word. I had noticed that both Golum and Bogey were still in the house. Typically, they would have been waiting for me on the patio with Renee. For some inexplicable reason, this time they'd been excluded.

As I opened the door and moved toward the chaise where Renee was seated, I saw her hands cupped around something so small I couldn't make it out. Must be the surprise, I guessed.

Good guess.

"Look at this precious kitty," Renee said, glowing like a new mother. "Isn't she cute?"

Cute isn't the term I would have chosen at that moment. The kitty looked like the *before* shot from one of those before-and-after commercials a pet grooming place might run. No, I'm being kind. She was underqualified for that picture. A chunk of hair was missing from her chest as though she'd been in a fight—and lost. What hair she had left was dirty and matted, and it appeared the poor thing hadn't eaten in days.

Actually, she'd eaten just a few hours earlier, thanks to *the Mother Teresa of catdom*. Before I could regain my composure enough to ask how this had happened, Renee volunteered the story.

"I was just leaving Dad's house when I found this straggly little kitty walking around in his garage," she said. Renee had spent the day visiting her father in the nearby town where he lived. "I knew Dad would feed the cat if it came around, but the poor thing was so emaciated I just had to bring her home and care for her. Isn't she sweet?"

As I said, marriage comes as a package— and I did like this package. Renee had come into my life at just the right time. She was exactly the right person.

What began as mutual attraction and friendship had matured into real love. Since meeting and marrying her, enthusiasm had returned to my life. Optimism had been reborn. The house had come alive again. The lights were burning brighter.

So, what could I say? What could I do?

In any event, I figured the adjustment would be easier for me than for Golum and Bogey. And it was. What began as an accommodation to Renee's inexplicable infatuation with cats evolved into my understanding and eventual genuine love for this particular cat, whom we named Zoey.

After a thorough examination by the vet, a *dipping* to make sure she was free of fleas, and a few weeks of special dietary care, Zoey began developing into one of the most beautiful creatures God ever created. It was hard for

Zoey

friends to believe this royal-looking pet had started life as a waif and stray. Most amazing, I was developing into a cat person.

Don't get me wrong. I'm as crazy about dogs as ever. Not even Zoey can take the place of that loyal, obedient, devoted and affectionate old Doberman, Golum. She'll never fill the gap left by our confident and funny little dachsie, Bogey. But she doesn't have to. Zoey has carved out her own spot. And, she's taught me much.

She's taught me that I can be both a dog person and a cat person. It doesn't have to be either/or. Just as I love my two children—

differently, but equally—so I've learned it isn't necessary to choose one or the other.

Zoey has taught me that I wasn't as free of prejudice and bigotry as I once thought—that I harbored a strong bias against all cats until this particular cat won my heart.

Zoey has taught me that I can change. Grow. Learn. That after all these years, I can still expand my horizons. Think differently. Open myself to new personalities and experiences.

I owe Renee a big *thank-you* for helping me see that if we want to be as terrific as our *dogs* think we are, it couldn't hurt to borrow a few qualities from our cats—such as independence, curiosity and playfulness.

I know Renee's pleased, overall, with my new attitude toward cats, but no doubt disappointed with what I've taught Zoey to do.

You see, I've trained her to come when I call and to jump up on my lap when I invite her.

"You know that's not supposed to happen," Renee frowns. "Cats are created to be independent. Cats should only come when *they* want to. They should only get on your lap when it's *their* idea.

"You've turned this wonderful cat into a dog."

Zoey should consider that a compliment!

Seven

Give and Take

The trouble with most of us is that we
would rather be ruined by praise
than saved by criticism.
—Norman Vincent Peale

Cat's motto: No matter what you've done
wrong, always try to make it look like the
dog did it.
—Unknown

When Bogey arrived at our home as a six-week-old puppy, he hadn't been housebroken.

Having read a few books and trained more than a few puppies, we understood that the process required both criticism and praise. If Bogey missed the papers we had spread out for him, he was to be corrected on the spot (so to speak).

But when he performed where he was supposed to, he was to be praised. This consistent balance between chastisement and approval would, ultimately, turn Bogey into a properly behaving dog. So it is with all of us.

A bruised ego can hurt worse than a broken bone.

I know. For a reporter and television news anchor, *ego injury* is a constant occupational hazard. The audience is never bashful about letting a newscaster know how the story could have been delivered better, written more accurately, presented more effectively—or, why it shouldn't have been aired at all.

Occasionally the criticism is extremely personal.

"Was the light out in your closet when you picked that horrendous tie?"

"Hope you didn't pay full price for that haircut."

"Where'd you ever get the idea that you're funny?"

"Better go on a diet, buddy. Didn't anyone ever tell you TV makes you look ten pounds heavier?"

Perhaps Andy Rooney was on target when he opined that ". . . the average dog is a nicer person than the average person."

Coaches know the feeling. On Monday morning, the fans all turn into quarterbacks, convinced they could have done it better than the coach did. They would have sent in the other running back sooner. They would have called that last play differently. They never would have gone with the quarterback the coach picked!

Of course, it isn't only broadcasters and coaches who attract critics. Anyone who attempts to do *anything* worthwhile should expect to become a target. Free advice, second-guessing and fault-finding not only are America's favorite pastime, they also are part of the price people pay to become leaders in any field. And that's okay. As Harry Truman once said, "If you can't stand the heat, get out of the kitchen."

What's important is that we learn to handle criticism in a healthy and productive way. That means, first, cultivating the ability to differentiate between constructive criticism that can help us and baseless criticism that may only get in our way.

I learned during my years in TV never to ignore any criticism without first examining it closely—even the very personal comments that stung my pride.

Rather than become defensive, perhaps I should examine the tie I wore for that broadcast; perhaps I should get a second opinion from my wife or a colleague. It's just possible that what looked good to me in the mirror didn't come off so well on camera.

And the haircut. Of course the caller may have been having a bad hair day herself and was just taking it out on me. But what do I have to lose by taking a closer look? Maybe my barber was the one having the bad day.

As for those one-liners, of course they aren't always sharp and on target. When you do 470 live broadcasts a year, adding up to more than 700 hours, not everything you ad lib is going to be Pulitzer Prize material. Nevertheless, maybe my comment tonight was *particularly* stupid—or inappropriate.

And my weight? Can't argue about that one. It's a constant battle.

Becoming as terrific as my dog thinks I am requires that I consider all criticism, sort out what's credible and learn from it. Kudos are more fun, but honest critiques are more helpful. Too many compliments may lull me into complacency. An occasional criticism keeps me grounded *and growing* if accepted graciously.

Presidents certainly know about criticism.

William Howard Taft, like all chief executives, had to endure his share of abuse from political opponents, voters and newspaper editorialists.

One evening at the dinner table, Taft's youngest son made a clearly disrespectful remark to him. Things got very quiet. The president looked thoughtful.

Finally, Mrs. Taft said, "Well, aren't you going to punish him?"

To which President Taft replied, "If the remark was addressed to me as his father, certainly he'll be disciplined.

"However, if he addressed it to me as President of the United States, that is his constitutional privilege."

We can't *grow* on a steady diet of nothing but criticism. Constant criticism shrivels the soul. We need encouragement, too.

Why is it we're so quick to find fault and so reluctant to praise? To be as good as our dog thinks we are, that has to be reversed. We need to become generous with encouragement but stingy with criticism. One of the most endearing qualities of a good dog is its capacity to comfort. To make us feel better. To *be there* as a friend and confidant.

During the final days of Nicki's life, our son

and daughter understandably were broken-hearted over their mother's illness.

Carey was sixteen, and the little dachshund she'd had since second grade provided some measure of comfort. More than once, I saw Carey take Bogey into her bedroom. Later, when I'd enter the room to turn out her light, Bogey would be nestled up to Carey as close as he could get. This four-legged friend never asked questions or tried to offer advice. The encouragement he provided transcended mere words. His love and caring didn't have to be spoken. They could be felt.

A few days after Nicki's death, the president of our company, Joel Chaseman, came to Detroit on one of his visits from Washington.

He walked into my office, placed his arm around my shoulders and just stood there. His only words were something like, "Mort, I'm sorry." But words weren't required.

Nothing he could have said would have encouraged me as much as his simple gesture of friendship, which let me know he cared.

No one is ever too big, too successful, too important to outgrow the need for encouragement, including one of pro football's all-time greats, Fran Tarkenton.

As we all know, quarterbacks don't block tacklers. However, the Minnesota Vikings were badly behind. They needed a surprise play. So, quarterback Tarkenton shocked his opponents by going in to block. His runner scored and the Vikings won.

The next day Tarkenton approached coach Bud Grant.

"Coach, you saw my block. How come you didn't say anything about it?"

Grant replied, "Sure, I saw the block. It was great. But you're always working hard out there, Fran. I figured I didn't have to tell you."

"Well," Tarkenton replied, "if you ever want me to block again, you do!"

People who are good at accepting criticism and good at giving praise invariably are good at something else: forgiving. It's another quality we can learn from our dogs. They don't hold grudges. Bogey could be scolded severely for getting into the garbage. He'd meekly accept the chastisement, fully understand our displeasure, but minutes later would be curled up on a lap with no hard feelings. Bogey could take his criticism from us one minute and offer encouragement to us the

next because he never became bitter or
resentful.

I once read that it's impossible for dogs to
develop ulcers. They can get a lot of other
things that afflict humans—but not an ulcer.
And I've always figured one reason for that is
dogs don't hold grudges. Refusing to let go of
an indignity, a slight or an insult is one of the
most destructive things we can do to ourselves. In time, it impacts both our physical
and our mental health.

A frontier preacher in Texas had been working hard to bring peace between cattle ranch-
ers and farmers. Finally he managed to get
the two sides together for a barbecue. When
they asked him to say the blessing, the old
preacher said: "Lord, give us the grace to bury
our hatchets—and the wisdom to forget where
we buried them. Amen."

Sometimes we adults hang on to emotional
baggage from childhood for which we feel
compelled, eventually, to ask forgiveness.

Ted called from his home in Kentucky to
tell his dad how sorry he was. The older man
was perplexed. What in the world had
prompted this sudden expression of regret?

Well, Ted explained, he'd been gluing tile on

the family-room floor and his seventeen-month-old son was helping.

"And Dad," he said. "It just made me think of all the times I'd helped you when I was little, and I just want to apologize."

Any healthy relationship involving any person—or any pet—requires an ongoing attitude of forgiveness. That's because neither humans nor animals will always behave exactly as we want them to 100 percent of the time.

Sometimes people come up with rather unique ways of dealing with disappointment in others.

When he was an army general, Dwight Eisenhower developed a habit which he carried with him into the White House as president.

Ike was determined not to let himself hate someone just because they'd insulted him or even taken some despicable action against him. He recognized that a grudge is an acid that first eats away at the container, and Ike refused to be such a container.

So he made it a habit of writing the offending individual's name on a piece of scrap paper, then dropping the paper into the lowest drawer of his desk, and saying to himself, "That finishes the incident, and so far as I'm concerned, that fellow." He said that over the years that drawer became sort of a private wastebasket for crumpled-up spite and discarded personalities. Best of all, it helped Ike avoid useless and self-destructive negative feelings.

Roderick McFarlane recalls something her grandmother told guests at her golden wedding celebration. This veteran of a fifty-year union said that on her wedding day she'd decided to make a list of ten of her husband's faults which, for the sake of their marriage, she would overlook.

As the guests were leaving, one young woman, whose own marriage had been in trouble, asked the grandmother what were some of those faults she'd decided to overlook.

With a twinkle in her eye, the elderly lady said, "To tell you the truth, dear, I never did get around to listing them. But whenever my husband did something that made me furious, I'd say to myself, 'Lucky for him that's one of the ten.'"

Yes, becoming as terrific as our dog thinks we are means learning to *give* and *take*.

To *give* encouragement.

To *take* criticism.

And to be as forgiving of others' mistakes as our dog is of ours.

Eight

The Hand That Feeds You

Two kinds of gratitude: The sudden kind we feel for what we take; the larger kind we feel for what we give.

—E. A. Robinson

Money will buy you a pretty good dog, but it won't buy the wag of his tail.

—Unknown

Not every dog is a good dog!

Let's face it. Even we dog lovers have to admit, some dogs are mean.

Porky was a mean dog. The meanest we ever owned and one of the most disagreeable I've ever met.

Porky would eat out of your hand, then bite you—a classic example of the dog that would "bite the hand that feeds him."

Renee once had a dog, Scruffy, that would lie on the couch with her, then bite her foot if she happened to get too close. He'd do the same with her children. Eventually, Scruffy had to find a new home.

Just like some people, some dogs will accept all the good things provided for them—food, shelter, companionship—without showing the slightest sign of gratitude.

Golum and Bogey, on the other hand, were models of thankfulness. They seemed genuinely appreciative for their good life. Consequently, we appreciated them.

We can't be as terrific as our dogs think we are until we cultivate an attitude of gratitude. Most of us understand and value this quality. That's why we work hard to instill it in our children. We explain to them the importance of thank-you notes when aunts, uncles or grandparents send a gift. We teach them to say "thank you" whenever someone opens a door for them or invites them to sit down. We recognize that not only is such an attitude morally right, it's crucial to their success in life.

People who are ungrateful are unpleasant to be around. They're the whiners, the complainers, the fault-finders who believe that behind every dark cloud there's an even darker one and behind that there's probably a tornado.

Renee and I were both fortunate to grow

up in homes where gratitude not only was a prevailing attitude, it required certain rituals, such as saying grace before meals. We were taught from childhood to appreciate the farmers who grew the food. The processors who packaged it. The hands that prepared it.

And most of all, to be grateful for the Creator who provided the sun, the soil, the rain and the seasons that made all of it possible.

In my work, I've traveled extensively. Visited many poor countries. Watched people struggle just to survive.

I've seen people in developing nations stand in long lines hoping that when they finally reached the sparsely stocked shelves, there'd be some sort of food left for them. I've watched parents agonize because there were no doctors to take care of their sick children.

Returning from these journeys, I'm always infused with a new sense of gratitude for all we have in the United States. How easily we Americans take for granted things that would be *luxuries* in many parts of the world: running water, electricity, adequate clothing, abundant food, cars, educational opportunities, medical care and jobs.

Then there are the intangibles: freedom to

speak our minds, to choose our leaders, to move from place to place, to marry the person of our choice and the freedom to worship. We exercise these freedoms often with hardly a thought as to how unique they are in the world.

We may on special occasions, such as Thanksgiving, think about how blessed we are. But unless we maintain a constant awareness of the unprecedented advantages we enjoy, we risk losing the capacity to be truly grateful.

Gratitude for what one has comes most easily to those who've not always had it. That's why it's difficult for many of us, raised in such a rich land, to fully and consistently appreciate our good fortune.

Those who immigrate here from the world's poverty pockets, from nations ruled by despots or ravaged by conflict, from places where starvation or prison are a daily possibility—such people have no difficulty being thankful.

A friend of mine who came here years ago from Greece runs a restaurant near the office where I used to work.

One evening as I was having dinner in his place, he came over to my table to say hello, and I complimented him on how well the business was doing.

"You certainly have worked hard to make it happen," I said.

He smiled, and responded, "There's nothing wrong with hard work. Yes, I put in fourteen or fifteen hours a day, but I'm so fortunate to have the opportunity this country has given me.

"My family is happy. I'm able to send my children to school so they can get an education and maybe not have to work so hard. But I have no complaints. I'm grateful."

As the son of a minister, I grew up in a home that was happy but certainly not affluent. We always had enough to eat, decent clothes to wear, and I never thought of us as *poor*. But we never were able to take the kinds of vacations my children now take for granted. For us, a major vacation was a two-week visit to my grandparents' house—by car.

To my children, a major vacation is a cruise on a luxury ship, a ski trip to the Canadian Rockies, a tour of Europe or a week at a rented condominium in the Caribbean.

I'm sure my children are grateful for the professional success we've enjoyed, the excellent schools they were able to attend and the head start in life all this has given them. But I know that, having never been without, it will be more challenging for them to develop the gratitude which comes naturally to those who haven't always had such advantages.

The good things we *receive* in life should produce gratitude. But there's an even deeper, more remarkable kind of gratitude: It's what we feel because of what we are able to *give*. The opportunity to share, to serve, to make a contribution—this produces in the human heart the most astounding gratitude of all.

There was an old farm couple in New England who knew something about *that* kind of gratitude. Samuel Walter Foss stumbled into it quite by accident.

He'd walked more than twenty miles in the New England sun and was tired.

Suddenly he spotted a shade tree. It looked so inviting. And from one limb there hung a sign: *There is a spring of water inside the fence. Drink if you are thirsty.*

Samuel walked around the fence and took a long, cool, refreshing drink. Then, next to the spring, he noticed a bench. And on it another sign: *Sit down and rest if you are tired.*

While sitting on the bench, Foss saw still

another sign—this one attached to a basket of apples: *If you like apples, help yourself.*

About that time, an old man walked up and Foss asked him to tell him about the signs.

"Well," the old gentleman explained. "We had the water going to waste. And my wife and I remembered an old bench we had up in the attic. And we have more apples this time of year than we can eat.

"So we put up the signs and they seem to be doing some little good."

Samuel Walter Foss thanked the man. Later that evening, Foss was inspired to write a poem which has become an American classic. It begins, "Let me live in a house by the side of the road and be a friend to man . . ."

Throughout our lives, you and I will have many regrets. We'll be sorry for things we said or failed to say. We'll be sorry for actions we took or failed to take. But there's one thing for which we'll never be sorry. We'll never regret that we were grateful.

Gratitude is like confetti: When you toss it around, some of it's bound to blow back on you.

Inevitably, someone reading this book is going to think, "Well, that all sounds very

nice. But what do I have to be grateful for?"
Everyone feels that way at times. Maybe your
marriage or your relationship is in shambles.
Or, you've just lost your job. Possibly you've
received a distressing medical report.

Life does get tough, and at times the problems pile on so thick that it's difficult to *see*
our blessings, let alone count them.

We may think, "I'll be grateful as soon as I
have something to be grateful about. Right
now, life stinks!" The irony is, it doesn't work
that way. Grateful people aren't grateful
because things are going great. It's the other
way around: Things always go *better* for the
person who's thankful!

As a reporter, I've interviewed hundreds—
perhaps thousands—of people at all levels of
life and in virtually all circumstances.

I've talked with families whose homes had
just been destroyed by a tornado. Others who'd
lost their houses to floods or fires.

I've spoken with parents devastated by the
tragic loss of a child. I've watched middle-
aged men despair because they'd been let go
from a job they believed was theirs for life
and felt their prospects for new employment
were virtually nonexistent.

In these and other sad circumstances, I noticed that some *victims* were able to cope much better than others. Why? What was the common denominator? Without exception, it was their sense of gratitude. Instead of focusing on what they'd lost, they concentrated on what they had left.

Without trying to gloss over the magnitude of their tragedy, they aimed toward the future. Their *thankful attitude* provided them with a resiliency that facilitated recovery. If the house was destroyed, well, they still had their health, their faith and each other. Somehow they would rebuild.

If their child had been taken, they'd cherish the memories and move ahead because, after all, that's what their child would have wanted.

If they'd lost a job, finding another might be difficult. But since there's no future in the past, they would look ahead, get busy, muster what resources they had and figure out something. The point is, these survivors, these people who showed the strongest coping mechanisms, were, without exception, people with a well-developed sense of gratitude.

Not only is gratitude a primary tool in rebuilding after disaster, it's fundamental to constructing happiness. Have you ever known anyone who was simultaneously happy and ungrateful?

Of course we've all known folks who seem to be grateful for their misery. Wallowing in their misfortune may provide them with their only joy. If you know people who take delight in their own wretchedness, please share with them the following:

TWENTY RULES TO MAKE
YOURSELF MISERABLE

1. Use the word "I" as often as possible.
2. Always be sensitive to slights.
3. Be jealous and envious.
4. Think only about yourself.
5. Talk only about yourself.
6. Trust no one.
7. Never forget a criticism.
8. Always expect to be appreciated.
9. Be suspicious.
10. Listen greedily to what others say of you.
11. Always look for faults in others.
12. Do as little as possible for others.
13. Shirk your duties if you can.
14. Never forget a service you've rendered.

15. Sulk if people aren't grateful for your favors.
16. Insist on consideration and respect.
17. Demand agreement with your own views on everything.
18. Always look for a good time.
19. Love yourself first.
20. Be selfish at all times.

While some may choose to follow the above formula, most of us prefer happiness to misery and peace of mind to inner anguish.

For us, there's no better starting point on the road to joy than gratitude.

Good dogs are grateful dogs.

They don't bite the hand that feeds them.

People who want to be as terrific as their dogs think they are don't either.

Nine

Lessons in Loyalty

(The Doberman pinscher) is ready, if need
be, to give prompt alarm and to back his
warning with defense of his master and his
master's goods. Yet, he is affectionate,
obedient and *loyal*.
—*Directory of Dogs*

Man is a dog's idea of what God should be.
—Holbrook Jackson

T hat description fits many breeds of dog. It certainly described our Doberman.

Golum was affectionate, obedient and usually gentle. But the moment he sensed that any member of the family might be in danger, his dark eyes narrowed, his steely strong body tensed, and he was ready to spring to our defense.

It happened rarely because it was rare for such a situation to develop. However, there was one time that Golum demonstrated just what he would do for us if called upon.

It was a cold, wintry day. We lived in a second-story condominium on a lake. Next to our building was an open peninsula that stretched about a half-mile into the water.

It was vacant land used mostly by fisher-men and other dog walkers like myself.

It was a perfect place to let a big dog like Golum run free for brief periods of time.

Always I would look around to make sure no one was on the peninsula who might be intimidated by the sight of a powerful Doberman on the loose. By now I was acquainted with most of the early-morning walkers, knew their dogs by name, and they all knew Golum.

This particular morning I made my usual survey of the scene, then unsnapped Golum's leash and watched him lope off toward the edge of the frozen lake. Within a minute or two, I spotted an old man making his way onto the peninsula from the other end. He was wearing a long coat that came nearly to his ankles, a scarf wrapped around his head and tied at the neck, and a wide-brimmed felt hat pulled down over the scarf. I had never seen him in the area before.

The man walked briskly toward me, and Golum must have seen him at about the same time I did.

Both Golum and the man reached me simultaneously and before I could order Golum to stop—before I could grab his collar to connect the leash—the old gentleman reached out his hand toward me and started to say something.

At that moment Golum sprang between us, grabbed the man's hand and held it in a vice-like grip until I could assure him that everything was all right.

The man was shaken, but unhurt. It all happened so fast, there was hardly time for either of us to react. Once Golum knew that this man meant no harm, he was calm.

I can't say the same for the man, but he seemed grateful to have escaped the encounter with nothing worse than tooth marks on his glove and he declined any further help from me. Lucky for us, there were no personal injury lawyers staking out the peninsula that morning.

Loyalty is a quality we all admire and one that sometimes seems in short supply these days. The fact that dogs score so high in the loyalty department may be a major reason we love them so much.

Over the years, newspapers have been filled

with accounts of loyal dogs performing the most heroic acts, responding quickly and appropriately in an emergency to save lives.

Dogs have pulled children from raging streams, extricated disabled people from wrecked cars or fires, taken bullets for their police handlers, and of course, we've all heard countless stories about dogs who trekked hundreds of miles to find their *lost* families.

In Japan, Hachi-ko's loyalty to his family has made him a legend, even though the golden-brown Akita has been dead more than sixty years. So powerful is his true-life story that it's known by virtually every Japanese schoolchild.

Songs and books have been written and at least one movie produced to celebrate Hachi-ko's incredible devotion to the university professor who owned him.

For years, Hachi-ko accompanied his master to the train station. Then, when the professor returned in the evening, the dog would be there waiting to accompany him on the walk home.

One day the professor suffered a heart attack at school and died. Hachi-ko, of course, was there to meet him. And, in fact, returned to that train station every morning and every evening for the next ten years, until the dog's death, hoping the professor would show up.

But we needn't look overseas to find remarkable stories of dog loyalty.

There's a memorial in Portland honoring Bobbie, a Scottish-collie mix who got separated from his family while they were visiting in Indiana. The family lived in Oregon and Bobbie spent the next six months making his way back to them.

He battled raging river rapids, endured the hardship of crossing the Rockies, and at one point he refused to stay with a family that wanted to adopt him. By the time Bobbie finally reached home, the pads of his paws were worn to the bone.

Can we ever be as terrific as our dog thinks we are without being as faithful as our dog? Many relationships today are based upon everything *but* loyalty. They can be predicated upon money, advantage, prestige or self-interest. But without a core of loyalty, relationships eventually come apart—business or personal.

"Two weeks ago, he would have done anything

for me," my friend said, referring to a long-time business associate.

"Now that I've lost my job, he won't even return phone calls."

I knew that this friend had held a high-profile, prestigious position. The other friend who now wouldn't return his calls had benefited greatly from the relationship.

My friend was hurt, not so much by the recent snub, but by his recognition that there hadn't really been a friendship at all.

He'd been *used*. The other man was his "friend" only as long as there was some monetary or business advantage in it for him.

"I know now who my *real* friends are," he continued. "They're the ones who would drive me to the airport at six o'clock in the morning. They're the ones who'll come in the middle of the night if I'm sick."

I have friends like that. One of them is Vince Leonard, a former colleague with whom I co-anchored the news in Philadelphia. What began as a strictly business relationship blossomed into a genuine friendship as we began to discover common interests and philosophies.

Vince and I were both pilots and for a period of time owned an airplane together.

One night as I returned home after delivering the eleven o'clock news, I began to feel a tightness in my chest.

Breathing was difficult. I was showing symptoms of a heart attack. I asked my wife to make two calls—the first to 911 and the second to Vince.

He was at our house before the ambulance arrived and ended up taking me to the hospital. Fortunately, there was no heart attack. The symptoms turned out to be stress-related and responded well to some lifestyle changes.

But it was comforting to know that in any emergency, I could count on Vince. He was more than a colleague and a partner in an airplane. He was a friend. He was loyal. He would *be there*.

I'm fortunate to have several friends like that—too many to list—friends I know will respond, whenever, whatever. Of course I've had other *acquaintances* in my life whose friendship was based upon considerations other than loyalty. Business friends. Social friends. Temporary friends such as those you meet on vacation or on a cruise. People whose company you enjoy and then never have occasion to contact again.

Usually, we know who our *real* friends are, the ones who will be loyal. We're not often surprised to learn that someone who pretended to be a friend was really just along for the ride, hoping to get something from us with no thought of reciprocating.

There's a story about an airline pilot announcing to his passengers: "The bad news is we've lost both our engines and we're going down.

"The good news is we're right over an island, and I'm confident I can land on it.

"The other bad news is this island is totally uncharted so it's not likely anyone will ever find us here."

A flight attendant noticed one passenger sitting calmly, reading his newspaper. She asked him how he could be so cool under the circumstances.

"No problem," he replied. "Yesterday I borrowed twenty thousand dollars from a friend back in Boston. I guarantee you *he'll* find me."

Loyal friends always have a way of finding us—not for what they can get from us, but for what they can give. Their allegiance springs not so much from what *we* are as from what *they* are. And loyalty is something that can't be dictated by decree nor enforced by contract. It has to spring from the heart.

Employers who choose not to be loyal to their workers will *never* be loyal no matter how many employment agreements are in place. Likewise, the worker who doesn't feel loyalty to his or her employer or job will *never* be loyal no matter how many letters of agreement have been signed.

Recently I attended an awards luncheon where a man was honored for having never missed a day's work in forty years. Not for illness. Not for a doctor's appointment. Not for any reason.

Every single day his boss—and his colleagues—knew he would be there. That kind of loyalty doesn't come from a contract. It comes from character.

As every good lawyer will tell you, the best-drawn legal document in the world has to float on a sea of goodwill. This is as true for business partnerships and marriages as it is for international peace agreements.

True loyalty can't be bought, and it can't be sold, even though some people are willing to put a price on it:

When the church secretary picked up the

phone she was startled to hear a countrified voice on the other end say, "I'd like to talk to the head hog at the trough."

As soon as she figured out that the man wished to speak to the senior pastor, the secretary was appalled. After all, she'd worked for the minister for ten years and was extremely loyal.

"Sir, you may not refer to our minister that way," she replied coolly.

"You may call him reverend. You may call him pastor. You may even call him brother. But you may not refer to him as the head hog at the trough."

After a slight pause, the voice on the other end said in a slow drawl, "Well, okay. I just wanted to donate ten thousand dollars to your church."

And the secretary replied, sweetly, "Can you hold, please? I think the big pig just walked through the door."

If you think loyalty's not so important, just think for a moment what life would be like if there were *no one* we could trust. I remember being on a news assignment in Poland before the collapse of communism when my hosts were terrified to talk about political matters anywhere except inside their car—with the radio turned up.

"We can't trust anybody," our English-speaking guide told me. "We don't know what rooms have been bugged or even who's on *their* side."

It was a terrible way to live. Trust, loyalty, knowing who we can depend upon—these are essential to a good life.

Like the other admirable qualities presented in this book, loyalty requires work. It doesn't happen automatically. Sometimes despite our best intentions, we let our friends down. Sometimes we fail our spouse or our children. Often we disappoint ourselves.

But without a strong sense of loyalty, without a determination to be faithful to those we love, to those we work for and who work for us, in a word, to those who depend upon us, we can't ever hope to be as terrific as our dog thinks we are.

Ten

The Play's the Thing

Be glad of life because it gives you the
chance to love and to work and to
play and to look at the stars.
—Henry Van Dyke

Every dog needs toys.
—*Dogs for Dummies*

Susie was a beagle. Well, mostly beagle as far as we could tell. While she was a "mix," she resembled the beagle line more than any other. Her temperament *definitely* was beagle—friendly, frisky and fond of playing.

Susie came into our lives shortly after Nicki and I married. Our first child wasn't born until eleven years later, so during that time Susie occupied a special, preeminent role in our household.

With no competition for our time and attention, Susie got to play with us a lot. I don't recall her having toys, other than a tug ring and a rubber squeak-plaything made to look like a shoe, but I do remember her great capacity to have a good time.

One of her favorite games was tugging on an old towel. When not in use, it stayed crumpled by her bed. Susie always knew when it was time to play. She'd grab the towel in her teeth, drag it over to whomever was closest, and begin shaking it back and forth. If that didn't get our attention, Susie would shake the towel again, this time adding a subtle but clearly audible *growl* for effect.

Dogs and children instinctively know how to play. Adults sometimes have to be retaught. It's sad when we allow the responsibilities of the *grown-up* world to suffocate our natural urge to have fun; we become so caught up on the treadmill of making a living that we forget to make a life.

A rancher had purchased some new custom boots, and, when they turned out to be too tight, the boot maker volunteered to stretch them. But the rancher said, "No, sir, not on your life. Every morning when I get out of bed I have to corral some cows that busted out the night before. Then I have to mend the fences they tore down.

"All day long I watch my ranch blow away in the dust. After supper, I turn on the news and have to hear how feed prices are up and beef prices are down.

"On top of that, my wife's always nagging me to move into town.

"No, sir, you're not stretchin' these boots. When I get ready for bed and pull 'em off, it's the only *real pleasure* I get all day!"

When the only pleasure we get out of life is an absence of pain, something's out of balance. My uncle used to tell a joke about a man who periodically banged his head against the wall simply because it felt so good when he stopped.

To derive the most from our play, it has to be more than merely the absence of work. Hooper, the dalmatian fire dog who lives at Engine Company 211 in Brooklyn, works hard during the day visiting schools with his handler, helping children develop an understanding of fire safety. You may have seen him on the *Late Show with David Letterman*.

But when Hooper's through with work, he doesn't just flop down on his bed at the fire station and vegetate. Before sleep comes play, and Hooper wants to run, roll around and generally have fun with his fire-fighting buddies.

In a world where too many have become

proverbial *couch potatoes*, it's interesting to observe that those with the most energy for *living* inevitably are those who expend the most energy *playing*.

Whether it's a round of golf, a game of tennis, a night at the bowling alley, an hour at the gym, it's not as important *which* activity we pursue as it is that we do *something*— something interesting, challenging and fun.

Just as children don't all enjoy the same games, we adults each have our own definition of fun. Many of my friends are golfers. I prefer tennis. Some are boaters. Renee and I enjoy boats, but prefer flying. There are as many ways to play as there are people who *need* to play. And *need* is the crucial word here. For the person who wishes to live a healthy, happy, well-rounded, satisfying life, play isn't optional.

The word *recreation* literally means to recreate. To rebuild our energy, our enthusiasm, our perspective. To redefine our priorities. Incorporating recreation into our lives requires incorporating it into our planning. No matter how much we enjoy a sport or a hobby, unless we build time for it into our schedules, it eventually will get crowded out of our lives. The merely important always loses to the immediately urgent.

One thing Renee and I consider great fun is an evening with friends. Our friends come in a variety of ages, races, philosophies, theologies and political persuasions, and we enjoy them all. But finding time for these pleasant get-togethers isn't easy.

Not so long ago, we were trying to arrange such an evening. *Coordinate our day planners*, as we call it. We proposed a couple of dates that worked for both Renee and me, but our friends already had plans.

A week later, after much juggling of four separate schedules, we finally found a date that would work for everybody. It was two months away.

Clearly it was time to stop, look and take stock of our lives. How had we come to this— our entire lives programmed into tiny squares in a daily date book? At the end of a day, or a year, or a lifetime, how many of those "important appointments" will really have been that important?

As I studied my own day planner, I wondered, "Where is the notation that says, *read a book*? Or the one committing me to *telephone a relative*

I haven't talked to in awhile? Or an entry to *take a walk, play tennis, write to a friend, go fishing?*" The pages and the hours were filled with work, with responsibilities, with obligations. But where on my calendar had I scheduled any fun?

Unfortunately, the frantic lives most of us lead these days leave little time for such activities unless we program them in. Yes, it is difficult. No, it is not impossible. If you think you can't do it, then ask yourself this question: What happened to your calendar the last time you had the flu?

The last time you were stranded at home by a blizzard? Or found your car broken down or the telephone not working for an entire day? Did the world stop? Did your life collapse? Did your office shut down? Well, if you run your own small business, maybe the office did close. But so what?

Wasn't it all there waiting for you to pick up and continue on with those *obligations* when you got back?

The problem is we don't place enough value on *play* to integrate it into our routines. To make it a top priority. The word itself conjures up images of children goofing off, of idle hours spent doing nothing important or worthwhile. Of course any child psychologist will tell you that play is extremely important—even vital—to the health and development of a child. It's just as important to the continuing well-being of adults.

Once when we'd returned from a three-week trip, our car, which was parked at the airport, wouldn't start. It didn't take a mechanical genius to figure out why: The battery had run down. Apparently a small light had been left on inside the car, and during those weeks it had slowly drained all the electrical power.

This can happen to us. If energy and enthusiasm are being drained out of our lives with no recharging going on, eventually none is left.

A car that's running can handle an incredible electrical load—lights, radio, air conditioner—but when the battery isn't being *recharged*, even a single, tiny light bulb is enough to deplete it.

Researchers at Philadelphia's Benjamin Franklin Clinic checked out the phenomenon of people being tired after a day's work. They discovered that most exhausted workers—especially those in business—share some common traits.

First, they pack up their workday troubles in their briefcase and bring them home every night.

These *tired* folks carry on business as usual during lunch instead of using the time to relax. Often they refuse to take vacations because of a belief that *they're indispensable*.

Most who complain of chronic exhaustion have no hobbies or recreational outlets. For them, it's all work and no play. If they do exercise or participate in a sport, they tend to overdo it—to bring the same, hard-driving, competitive spirit to the pursuit as they bring to the office.

To be effective in relieving stress and reinvigorating us, play should never be work. Have you ever seen a golfer or a tennis player attack the game with such intensity you just knew they couldn't possibly be having fun? Or watched a jogger pounding the pavement with the grim expression of a mortician?

George Carlin said he'd take up running just as soon as he passed a jogger who was *smiling*.

Dogs and children know that play is supposed to be fun. They understand that the purpose of a game is not to see how fast it can be completed.

But we adults are so accustomed to doing everything in a hurry, we allow this unhealthy syndrome to seep into our recreation.

Entrepreneurs these days are making tons of money selling devices designed solely to save time—everything from radar detectors to microwave ovens to high-speed computer modems.

We'll pay thirty times the price of postage to insure next-day delivery whether such dispatch is required or not.

We'll phone when we could as easily write. We'll fly when driving might make more sense—but of course, cars take longer.

In business, time is money and sometimes the cost-benefit ratio favors speed over expense. But the *business of living* is something else. Jeffrey Hackler wrote to the *Brown University Alumni Monthly*, describing a week-long walking tour he'd made on the Japanese island of Shikoku. He wanted to visit as many of the temples as he could.

After two days, Jeffrey called a friend in Japan to brag about how fast he was traveling from one temple to the next. The man's response brought Jeffrey up short:

"It's not *getting to the temple* that counts," he said. "It's the walk."

The next day Jeffrey paid more attention to the walk itself. He began to enjoy the flowers, the rivers, the forests. He felt the air; he slowed down.

It dawned on him that for much of his life he had erected his own temples, his own goals, then tried to reach them as quickly as possible. Now he was learning, it's *the walk* that counts!

Satchel Paige once warned, "Never look back, somethin' may be gainin' on you." But if we never slow down, something good may never catch up to us.

Several times over my career, I've been sent to Latin America on news assignments.

There's a custom that persists south of the border which I think should be imported to the United States. It's called siesta, a midday time-out when stores close, commerce stops and shopkeepers rest. I understand not all of them use the time to actually nap these days. Apparently, some have become so American-ized that they use the siesta to catch up on paperwork in the back room.

But the siesta is a wonderful concept. History, medical science and common sense are all plainly on the side of this custom.

John D. Rockefeller lived to be ninety-eight and claimed that taking a half-hour nap every day at noon contributed to his longevity.

Thomas Edison took frequent catnaps throughout the day and said they were greatly responsible for his remarkable energy. Those naps may also explain how Edison got by on only three or four hours of sleep each night.

Connie Mack, who also lived to a ripe old age, took a nap before every ballgame.

When Henry Ford was asked late in life how he accomplished so much, he replied, "I never stand up when I can sit down, and I never sit down when I can lie down." Our dogs would have understood that philosophy. Every one of them lived by it.

A man and his wife in Phoenix were cleaning out their garage one Saturday when a Japanese couple stopped in front of the open door and asked if they could take a picture.

The couple agreed, but they were curious. Both were dressed in their jeans and were standing there, up to their ears in clutter. Why did these foreign visitors find them such interesting subjects?

As the Japanese gentleman raised his camera, he explained quietly, "Our son is thinking of moving to the United States. We want to send him pictures of Americans relaxing on the weekend."

To be as terrific as our dog thinks we are, we must learn to play. To pace ourselves. To relax.

After all, we don't quit playing because we grow old.

We grow old because we quit playing.

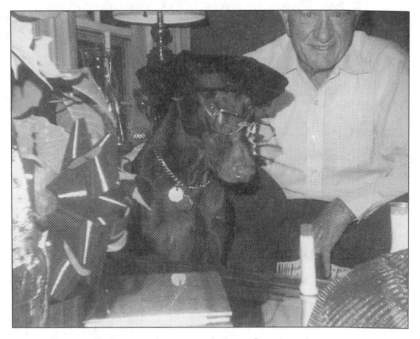

Golum and my stepfather, Guy Lambert

Eleven

Old Dogs, New Tricks

A well-trained, grown-up dog is a pleasure to have around the house. He knows the rules and obeys them.

—Louis Sabin

I call my dog Spot. *He's* really all just one color, but you should see my *rug*.

—Bob Orben

Golum was full grown and well-trained when he came into our lives. The college student, who first found this Doberman as a puppy wandering along a road, had done a fine job of guiding him to maturity as a true gentleman.

He'd also taught him several charming tricks. Golum shook hands with either paw upon verbal command. He knew his left from his right. But to me, his most endearing performance was when he would sit as still as a statue after a dog biscuit had been placed on his nose.

Golum would balance the biscuit, without wincing a single one of his powerful muscles, until permission was given to move. As soon as I said, "Okay, Golum," he'd flip the biscuit into the air and catch it in his mouth.

He never seemed to tire of this routine, and we never tired of initiating it to show friends how clever Golum was.

Young dogs learn easily. With understanding and patience, they can be taught remarkable and sophisticated skills, far beyond the more common feats of heel, sit, lie and roll over. We're all familiar with the incredible way guide dogs become *eyes* for their blind masters. Recently dogs also have shown an amazing talent as ears for the hearing impaired.

Of course, for centuries dogs have been trained to pull sleds in Alaska, herd sheep and cattle, rescue hunters trapped on mountains and guard both people and property. The reason dogs are able to accomplish all of these missions is because they're *teachable*. And contrary to the popular myth, most dogs never totally lose this capacity. You really *can* teach an old dog new tricks.

To be as terrific as our dog thinks we are, we, too, must remain teachable. Always. As long as we live. We have to rid ourselves of this notion that learning happens in school and once we're through with that, we're through. Graduation ceremonies are called commencements precisely because they represent a commencing—*a beginning*—not a conclusion. They may mark the end of school, but they should represent the start of education.

School doesn't teach us what we need to know to deal with life so much as it teaches us *how to learn* what we need to know. And the learning process should never stop.

When he was well along in years, Albert Einstein found himself seated next to a young college student at a dinner party. The student failed to recognize the great scientist and to make conversation, he asked, "What would you say is your profession?"

Einstein replied, "I devote myself to the study of physics."

To which the student replied,

"You mean you're still studying physics at your age? I finished that last semester!"

Unlike that naive student, Einstein, one of the greatest minds of the twentieth century, understood that one can never know everything about anything—that even a brilliant scientist has to continually study and learn.

It is the workers who remain *teachable* that are surviving and even *thriving* in today's rapidly changing job environment. The breathtaking rate at which technology and downsizing are changing the workplace has created a new axiom in the marketplace: *Only the flexible survive*. Those who can't or won't remain pliable—teachable—are destined to be broken by today's economic forces.

This principle is quite apparent in the world of physics. As a news reporter, I've covered more than one story where an infant was the only survivor of a car wreck or a plane crash. I recall one incredible account of a toddler falling from a five-story window and surviving with only a few cuts and bruises.

Why? Because babies don't tighten up. Their bodies don't become rigid in the face of challenge. Because they remain flexible, they're often able to survive an impact that would be fatal to a tensed-up adult.

While serving in the Strategic Air Command, I learned something quite interesting about our B-52 bombers. These behemoths of the sky have wings so flexible their tips move up and down during flight more than thirty feet. This flapping motion, which isn't detectable to the eye, is essential to keep the wings from breaking under the stress of nearly half a million pounds.

Flexibility is a key to survival and success. Dale Carnegie used to keep an old sock on his desk just to remind him of how limp he needed to be. It prompted him to relax. To roll with the punches. To stay flexible.

When we stop being teachable, we stop altering our opinions. And opinions should be subject to adjustment as we acquire new knowledge. When we refuse to consider new ideas we stunt our own growth. We halt our own progress.

Inflexible people also tend to have higher blood pressure, more heart attacks and other stress-related illnesses. Flexible—*teachable*—people are healthier, happier people.

In Rocky Ford, Colorado, an older woman sat on the floor to play paper dolls with her granddaughters. She has a touch of arthritis and is a bit overweight, so assuming this position wasn't easy. But she decided it was worth it when one of the little girls said to her, "Grandma, I'm glad you know how to bend."

Age may stiffen our joints. It doesn't have to harden our attitudes. At home or on the job, there are six words that can bring progress to a screeching halt. The words are: *We've always done it this way!* Whenever anyone pulls out that old chestnut in response to some new idea, watch out. Such people seem oblivious to the fact that the way it's being done now— *the way we've always done it*—was itself an innovation at one time. Somebody, at some time, had to do it *that* way for the very first time.

Can't you hear some traditionalist objecting to the first book with the observation, "Don't know why we have to turn pages when we've always gotten along with scrolls. Rolling must be better than turning because *we've always done it this way*."

Or how about, "I don't see why you want to put the bathroom indoors. Outdoor privies must be just fine because *we've always done it this way*."

An executive was scheduled to address a formal banquet and was nearly ready when the host of the event showed up at his hotel room to drive him to the affair.

But the executive was having some difficulty tying his bow tie. "My wife usually ties this for me," he explained to his host. "But she couldn't come on this trip. Do you think you could help?"

"No problem," the man at the door replied. "I'm good at tying bow ties, but you will have to lie down on the bed because I'm a funeral director and that's the only way I know how to do it."

Often the way *we've always done it* is the only way we know. But clinging to a procedure or a process simply out of habit isn't the *only* indicator that we've lost *our teachability*. Six other gauges may suggest a hardening of the attitudes:

1. We're not ready for that yet.
2. We're doing all right without it.
3. We tried it once, and it didn't work out.
4. It costs too much.
5. That's not our responsibility.
6. It won't work.

If we find ourselves routinely throwing up these *reasons* for maintaining the status quo, then we might want to reexamine our *teachability*. When we have a high teachability quotient, we're excited by new ideas. We're eager to learn, to grow, to take advantage of the incredible opportunities created by change.

This is not to suggest that change is easy, even when we recognize its value and welcome it.

After the decision was made several years ago to computerize our TV newsroom, there was much consternation among some of the old veteran journalists. I must confess, I had serious reservations about my ability to master the new technology after years of plunking away on a typewriter.

However, I remembered how strange the new *electric* typewriters had felt when they first arrived to replace our antiquated, manual machines. Those old finger-pushers had served us well since my first days as a cub reporter.

I recalled that within a very short time, the electric typewriters had proven themselves so much faster and easier that none of us would have ever considered going back to the manual machines. (Didn't we go through the same process with power steering and power brakes on our cars?)

Well, it didn't take our newsroom long to adapt to the new computer technology and, almost as quickly, become addicted to it.

As I write this book—on my computer, with

its automatic spell-check, its built-in dictionary and thesaurus, its willingness to let me quickly and easily move entire paragraphs or pages around—I can't imagine returning to any typewriter, manual or electric. It would feel like chiseling words onto stone tablets. Every hour that I spend writing now would take a day.

There's always some discomfort, even pain, associated with change. That includes change which, ultimately, is for the better:

Once when my tennis instructor showed me an improved way to hold my racquet, I found his method most uncomfortable. Early on, it made my swing worse. But, eventually, as I got accustomed to the new grip, my swing improved considerably. In order to improve, I had to give up the familiar and accept some pain in the process.

Sometimes we cling to the tried and true because it's easier. Sometimes, because we're afraid that if we try to change, we'll mess up. We do things a certain way because it's the only way we *can* do them with certainty.

A family had recently moved into the neighborhood when the little girl overslept one morning and missed her school bus. The father said he'd drive her to school if she'd show him the way.

After traveling several blocks, she told him to turn right. Then, a few blocks later, turn left. Another left and two rights finally brought them to the school. But as they arrived, dad recognized that they were only a couple of blocks from their house.

"Why did you take us so far out of our way?" he asked the little girl.

"Because, Dad," she said, "that's the way the school bus goes, and it's the only way I know."

How many tasks are we performing the hard way simply because it's the only way we know?

How many problems are we failing to solve because we haven't been *teachable*, haven't been willing to seek out solutions that would work!

This much is certain: If we continue doing what we've been doing, we'll continue getting the results we've been getting. It may sound like stating the obvious, but often we're slow to understand this truth: There's no real change without *change*.

Life definitely is a fast-track these days. Lee Iacocca acknowledged this when he said,

"Either lead, follow or get out of the way." He might have added, "If you don't make dust, you eat dust."

One good way to be as terrific as our dog thinks we are is to be as *willing* as our dog to learn new tricks. Flexible people, like teachable dogs, fit in better, get ahead faster, make friends easier, feel better about themselves and their environment and, generally, have more fun.

And, as any well-trained pooch can tell you, learning to do new tricks can get you some really neat treats.

Twelve

An Airtight Box

We are here and it is now. Further than that, all knowledge is moonshine.
—H. L. Mencken

A dog lives in the now. Just as he doesn't reflect on his past, he can't imagine his future.
—*Dogs for Dummies*

So far we've considered things dogs *do* that make them good role models for humans.

We've looked at canine characteristics that could help make us as terrific as our dog thinks we are.

We've discussed the enthusiasm of dogs, their optimism, acceptance, gratitude, loyalty, playfulness and teachability.

Now let's look at something dogs *cannot* do —something they *cannot* and we *need not* do: A dog can't regret the past or fear the future. A dog can *only* live in the *now*.

In her helpful handbook, *Dogs for Dummies*, author Gina Spadafori says:

Your dog doesn't know he's getting older. His gray hairs concern him not, nor does he worry about the other visible effects of time, the thickening of his body, the thinning of his limbs. He doesn't count the number of times he can fetch a ball before tiring and compare that to his performance when he was a young dog in his prime.

When we attended New York's Marble Collegiate Church in the mid-sixties, the late Dr. Norman Vincent Peale delivered a particularly powerful sermon one Sunday morning which has influenced me over these past three decades. He titled it: "Live Your Life in an Airtight Box."

Sounds a bit uncomfortable, doesn't it? The truth is, there's no way to live life comfortably *except* inside an airtight box. The box is *today*. Dr. Peale urged us to keep *today* so tightly sealed off from yesterday and tomorrow that neither past mistakes nor future dangers can seep in and spoil it.

He didn't suggest that we *ignore* wrongs committed in the past or that we fail to learn from them. He didn't tell us to make no plans or take no precautions for the future.

His point was that unless we determine to live here and now with the opportunities and promises of *this moment*, we'll never find any joy in life.

Guilt and anxiety will rob us not only of happiness, but also of our ability to deal constructively with all of life's challenges.

Dr. Peale noted that Jesus had instructed his disciples to *take no thought for tomorrow* because even the birds and the flowers get along quite nicely without worrying. Everything they need is provided for them.

Mark Twain, in his later years, observed that he was an old man who'd seen lots of trouble—most of which never happened. Anxieties about the future will pollute the atmosphere of today just as surely as will regrets about the past.

Certainly past mistakes should not be trivialized. Not everything we've done in the past can be *ignored*. Some of our more serious misdeeds may have to be dealt with before it's okay to forget them. We may recognize a need to ask forgiveness from God or from those who've been hurt by our actions. Once appropriate amends have been made, we need to *let go* of the past and refuse to let it spoil the present. What's done can't be *un*done. But why let the past *un*do *us* and sabotage *today's* best intentions?

Dogs don't do that. They have a way of learning from their errors without brooding over them. I can't imagine Golum and Bogey lying in front of our fireplace, unable to enjoy the warmth and peacefulness of the moment because they were so wracked with guilt over something they'd done earlier in the day.

Dogs know how to deal with mistakes, accept their scoldings, then move on.

I also suspect our dogs never allowed the prospect of a next day's visit to the vet to spoil the pleasure of *today*. They could do their shaking and trembling en route. Tomorrow would be soon enough to whine. Why make *this day* miserable with anxious anticipation?

And they certainly didn't lie around anticipating what illnesses they might contract in the future. Have you ever heard of a dog that was a hypochondriac?

Scratching the flea that's biting *now* is sufficient for any dog. Why should they get all worked up about the heartworm that might be discovered tomorrow, or the icky medicine they might be forced to take next week?

I once knew of a television executive who would rush into his doctor's office for electrocardiograms two or three times a month. He was abnormally frightened of having a heart attack even though all of his risk factors were within the normal range. He allowed so much of *tomorrow's* frightening possibilities to seep into his *todays* that he never really enjoyed them.

It's been my observation that people who attain a peaceful and happy old age are those who have not been chronic worriers. Growing old clearly brings with it legitimate concerns.

Will the money last as long as I do? What happens if I become disabled? Where will I go when I can no longer live in my house? Will I eventually be left alone? But excessive anxiety doesn't change the future. It only corrupts the present.

Not many of us enjoy the financial security George Burns had, but we would all be *richer* if we adopted his attitude toward the future. Until he died at age 100, Burns was too busy *living today* to *worry about tomorrow*.

Asked why, with all his wealth and success

in show business, he hadn't retired, Burns once told a reporter:

"If I had started slowing down when I was sixty-five or seventy, by now I'd be stopped. A turtle would move faster.

"But I didn't slow down. I kept going. And now there isn't a turtle around that can pass me."

By living each day to the fullest without borrowing either past or future troubles, George Burns showed the world that even if we can't stop the clock, we can keep winding it up again.

At every stage in life, we're faced with specific challenges; if we're prudent, we deal with them. Living in an airtight box doesn't mean sealing out *reality* or refusing to prepare for the future. But there's a difference in preparing for tomorrow and permitting potential problems to spoil *today*. Just as we can't *re*live yesterday, we can't *pre*live tomorrow.

At the time the movie *Apollo 13* was being released, I hosted a news conference for astronaut Jim Lovell, commander of that ill-fated flight. One of the reporters asked Lovell if he'd been worried after the explosion that almost cost all three crew members their lives.

Lovell said, "No, frankly, worry is a useless emotion. I was too busy *fixing* the problem to worry about it." Lovell, literally and figuratively, was living at that moment in an airtight box.

He didn't have time or the inclination to regret past mistakes that he, his crew or ground technicians might have made. Fretting over how it might have been different was futile.

He didn't have time or the inclination to worry about what might happen if they couldn't fix it. Jim Lovell and his teammates sealed off the past and the future, lived fully in the present, and all three of them survived because of it.

There's a story about a would-be skydiver who'd arrived at his moment of truth. He had dreamed about this day. Trained vigorously for it. But as he crouched in the airplane's open door, clutching desperately, refusing to let go, he simply couldn't bring himself to jump.

Finally, he heard his instructor's reassuring voice just behind him.

"Look at it this way. If your chute opens and you land successfully, you have nothing to worry about.

"And if it fails to open and you smash into the ground and die, you have nothing to worry about."

There really is nothing for us to worry about because, as Jim Lovell recognized, worry is a useless emotion. If we use today to the fullest, take advantage of the opportunity it provides to compensate for past failures and to prepare for future needs, then we don't need to waste energy regretting or fearing.

One way to be as terrific as our dog thinks we are is to seal ourselves inside an airtight box called *today*. But if we're in an airtight box, what can we breathe? The answer is *hope*. It's oxygen for the soul.

According to Father James Keller, founder of The Christophers:

> Hope looks for the good in people instead of harping on the worst.
>
> Hope opens doors where despair closes them.
>
> Hope discovers what can be done instead of grumbling about what cannot.
>
> Hope draws its power from a deep trust in God and the basic goodness of human nature.

Hope lights a candle instead of cursing the darkness.

Hope regards problems, small or large, as opportunities.

Hope cherishes no illusions, nor does it yield to cynicism.

Hope sets big goals and is not frustrated by repeated difficulties or setbacks.

Hope pushes ahead when it would be easy to quit.

Could there possibly be *anything* better to breathe inside the airtight box of *today* than the pure, refreshing, healing atmosphere of *hope?*

Father James Keller's words on hope reprinted by permission of The Christophers.

READER/CUSTOMER CARE SURVEY

If you are enjoying this book, please help us serve you better and meet your changing needs by taking a few minutes to complete this survey. Please fold it and drop it in the mail.

As a special "**Thank You**" we'll send you news about new books and a valuable **Gift Certificate!**

PLEASE PRINT C8C

NAME:_____

ADDRESS: _____

_____

TELEPHONE NUMBER: _____

FAX NUMBER: _____

E-MAIL: _____

WEBSITE: _____

(1) Gender: 1)_____Female 2)_____Male

(2) Age:
1)_____12 or under 5)_____30-39
2)_____13-15 6)_____40-49
3)_____16-19 7)_____50-59
4)_____20-29 8)_____60+

(3) Your Children's Age(s):
Check all that apply.
1)_____6 or Under 3)_____11-14
2)_____7-10 4)_____15-18

(7) Marital Status:
1)_____Married
2)_____Single
3)_____Divorced/Wid.

(8) Was this book
1)_____Purchased for yourself?
2)_____Received as a gift?

(9) How many books do you read a month?
1)_____1 3)_____3
2)_____2 4)_____4+

(10) How did you find out about this book?
Please check ONE.
1)_____Personal Recommendation
2)_____Store Display
3)_____TV/Radio Program
4)_____Bestseller List
5)_____Website
6)_____Advertisement/Article or Book Review
7)_____Catalog or mailing
8)_____Other_____

(11) What FIVE subject areas do you enjoy reading about most?
Rank: 1 (favorite) through 5 (least favorite)
A)_____ Self Development
B)_____ New Age/Alternative Healing
C)_____ Storytelling
D)_____ Spirituality/Inspiration
E)_____ Family and Relationships
F)_____ Health and Nutrition
G)_____ Recovery
H)_____ Business/Professional
I) _____ Entertainment
J) _____ Teen Issues
K)_____ Pets

(16) Where do you purchase most of your books?
Check the top TWO locations.
A)_____ General Bookstore
B)_____ Religious Bookstore
C)_____ Warehouse/Price Club
D)_____ Discount or Other Retail Store
E)_____ Website
F)_____ Book Club/Mail Order

(18) Did you enjoy the stories in this book?
1)_____Almost All
2)_____Few
3)_____Some

(19) What type of magazine do you SUBSCRIBE to?
Check up to FIVE subscription categories.
A)_____ General Inspiration
B)_____ Religious/Devotional
C)_____ Business/Professional
D)_____ World News/Current Events
E)_____ Entertainment
F)_____ Homemaking, Cooking, Crafts
G)_____ Women's Issues
H)_____ Other (please specify) _____

(24) Please indicate your income level
1)_____Student/Retired-fixed income
2)_____Under $25,000
3)_____$25,000-$50,000
4)_____$50,001-$75,000
5)_____$75,001-$100,000
6)_____Over $100,000

FOLD HERE

((25) Do you attend seminars?
1)_____Yes   2)_____No

(26) If you answered yes, what type?
Check all that apply.
1)_____Business/Financial
2)_____Motivational
3)_____Religious/Spiritual
4)_____Job-related
5)_____Family/Relationship issues

(31) Are you:
1) A Parent?_____
2) A Grandparent?_____

Additional comments you would like to make:

_____
_____
_____
_____

N-CS

C8C

Thirteen

Scratch That Itch

I am convinced that basically dogs think
humans are nuts.
—John Steinbeck

If one advances confidently in the direction
of his dreams, and endeavors to live the life
he has imagined, he will meet with a success
unexpected in common hours.
—Henry David Thoreau

A dog knows there's only one way to handle an itch: scratch it.

And when a dog wants something, he goes after it. Period.

We humans, on the other hand, will let an *itch* aggravate us for years without addressing it. We may *itch* to learn a new skill, break a bad habit, start a business, finish college, move to another town or begin a new relationship. But unlike our dog, we don't always *go for it*. Itches that aren't scratched become a real annoyance, which is why dogs refuse to put up with them.

It isn't only chiggers and fleas that will prompt a dog to scratch. Dogs will scratch *any* kind of itch. They never hesitate to go after *what* they want.

Whether Bogey spotted a bone in the alley, a cat on the neighbor's porch or an appealing female dog in the next yard, he never hesitated to pursue the object of his interest. Promptly and with gusto. (Admittedly, after the veterinarian performed a certain, routine function on his libido, Bogey seemed more attracted to bones and cats than to female dogs.)

The point is, Bogey—like all dogs—knew what was important to him and enthusiastically went after it.

One of Golum's favorite activities was chasing other dogs just for the fun of it. He never attacked. Instead, he merely danced around, sniffing, whining, dipping down on his front paws, wagging his stub and generally doing all those strange things dogs understand as part of their *let's-get-to-know-each-other-better* ritual. But meeting dogs was a passion with Golum, and whenever he saw a new one on our peninsula, it required all the strength I could muster to hold him back.

That was something I forgot to mention to Silvia. She was my secretary and often worked at the office we maintained in our home. On this particular wintry day, I was on the telephone when Golum signaled that he wanted out. Silvia volunteered.

My quick advice was simply, "Silvia, be careful out there. There's ice under the snow."

Now Silvia is a woman of many talents and a variety of interests—weight lifting and wrestling *not* being among them.

Within minutes of hearing the front door close, I heard a loud, helpless shout coming from the peninsula.

It was more of a shriek, and while it included some words I didn't know Silvia knew, the desperate sounds were, unmistakably, coming from Silvia.

I arrived at the window just in time to see this woman, encased in a heavy coat befitting an Eskimo, down flat on her stomach, hanging on to Golum's leash for dear life, and being dragged along through the snow like an Iditarod driver who'd lost his sled and didn't know it.

It was clear Golum had sighted a new dog on his grounds and was determined to break loose and initiate an introduction. Silvia, resolute lady that she is, was just as determined to stop him. While nobody, including Golum, ever had more tenacity than Silvia, it was obvious that raw muscle was deciding *this* test of wills.

How much we could all accomplish if we'd just be as bold as our dogs in going after what we want. Of course this doesn't mean just *anything* we want. Some things we *think* we want may not be in our own best interest.

They may be ill-advised, immoral, illegal or impossible. Itches ought to be evaluated to determine whether they're worth scratching. While it takes determination to *reach* goals, it takes judgment to *establish* the right ones.

There was a man in a small community out West who was bragging to a friend that his dog could whip any dog in town.

About that time, his mutt spotted another, much bigger dog, and took out after him. The bigger dog made quick work of his attacker, sending the little guy whimpering back to his master.

"I thought you said your dog could whip any dog in town?" the friend laughed.

"Well, he can," the embarrassed owner of the dog replied. "He's a real good fighter. But

I gotta admit, sometimes he's a lousy judge of dogs!"

Before we take off to fight, we need to analyze the objective and compute the cost. Before pursuing a dream the way Golum shot off across that peninsula, we need to carefully examine the dream. Is it a goal that's worthy of our commitment? Does it deserve the time, energy, effort and money it may require? If it does, then *go for it*!

Too often, instead of scratching our itch, we talk ourselves into believing it's no longer there. Or we tell ourselves, it wasn't important in the first place.

Do we let ourselves off the hook, settling for what's easy and available instead of holding out for what we really want? Do we compromise our dreams because surrender seems preferable to hard work and sacrifice?

This is not to say dreams shouldn't change or that goals shouldn't be adjusted. They should. But sometimes we give up too easily on an objective that was really important to us, not because we no longer care, but because we're no longer willing to persevere. Often we'll trade in our big dreams for small ones, forgetting that we never grow to be any greater than our vision.

I have a friend in Florida, Gene Pontius, who raises koi, those colorful Japanese carp, which come in seemingly endless sizes, shades and designs.

Gene told me something about these popular fish that I never knew: If you place koi minnows in a small fish bowl, they'll grow to be only two or three inches long. Then, growth stops.

Place them in a larger tank and they may reach six to ten inches. Put koi in a pond, they can grow as long as a foot and a half. But, place them in a huge lake, and koi can reach lengths up to three feet.

The size of the fish is determined by the size of the environment. So, too, the size of our accomplishments in life is determined by the size of our dreams.

It's been said, "The saddest words of tongue or pen are these—it might have been." Few things are more tragic than to see someone with talent, ability and potential, end up short of his or her dreams simply because the person couldn't find the internal fortitude to press on. When the going got tough, they got out.

The late Father William Cunningham was

a warm and wonderful priest who founded Detroit's *Focus Hope*. That organization has won international acclaim for training at-risk young people for today's and tomorrow's job markets. Earlier in his career, Father Cunningham had taught English in a Jesuit High School. One of his students, a man who's now quite successful in business, recently told me the story of Father Cunningham's response to one of his speech assignments.

The priest said, "Joe, I'm giving you an A for the great voice God gave you. I'm giving you an F for the way you've failed to use it. That averages out to a C, and that's the grade you're getting."

In the mid 1960s, I attended a farewell party for Peter Jennings. The popular anchor of ABC's nightly network newscast was at that time a very young correspondent, like most of us attending the event.

It was hosted by Ted Koppel and his wife, Grace Ann.

Ted and I were correspondents with ABC's radio network, as were many of the friends gathered that evening including Steve Bell, Ron Cochran, Roger Sharp and Don Farmer. What struck me most about the affair was

Jennings's positive, upbeat attitude.

He was just coming off one of the toughest, most impossible assignments in network television: At age twenty-six he had been put in ABC's prime anchor chair to compete with veteran newsmen Chet Huntley and David Brinkley on NBC and the venerable Walter Cronkite on CBS.

Peter was bright, charming, witty and a solid journalist. But he was young and relatively inexperienced. The trade press had, from the beginning, predicted disaster.

Now, Peter had been replaced, and initially there was much speculation as to how he would handle his tumble and where he'd land. No one doubted that, wherever he hit, he'd land on his feet. Several major market TV stations were anxious to hire him.

But Jennings had a different agenda. A different goal. He would stay with ABC, accept a foreign assignment—no doubt at considerably less money—and prove to the world what a capable, determined newsman he really was.

Peter Jennings had an itch to be back in that anchor chair, someday. He understood the cost. He accepted the challenges. He paid the price. And now, more than thirty years later, the itch definitely has been scratched.

A few years ago, I emceed a luncheon honoring Heather Whitestone, the 1995 Miss America. Sitting next to her during lunch, I was deeply impressed by her charisma, her leadership skills, her commitment to helping others. Heather proved to be both inspired and inspiring. Within a minute or two of conversing with her, one became virtually oblivious to the fact that Heather is deaf.

She's a good lip reader and has a marvelous sense of humor to go with the skill. At one point, Heather told me about making a joint appearance with then-President George Bush, not long after he'd made his now famous no-new-taxes remark, challenging a reporter to "read my lips."

When the program chair got up to introduce Heather, he turned to George Bush and said, "Mr. President, here's someone who really *can* read your lips."

I asked Heather how much of a disadvantage her disability had been during the years she was entering pageants leading up to the Miss America contest. Her reply was interesting:

"You know, Mort, there was a real advantage

to being deaf. I was never able to hear all those people telling me I couldn't do something. That I could never become Miss America. That I couldn't realize my dream."

That's certainly part of the secret to scratching our itches in life—turning a *deaf ear* to the cynics, the critics, the pessimists who try to tell us we'll never make it.

Every goal I've reached, every dream I've realized, happened in spite of the skeptics. Maybe it was partly *because* of them. No doubt I was spurred on and motivated by the naysayers, who were convinced I could not succeed. I've always been grateful to family and friends for encouraging me and believing in me. But perhaps I owe a similar debt of gratitude to the doubters.

One reason I write motivational books and air daily motivational radio programs is because I know, firsthand, that goals *can* be reached.

If this preacher's kid from a small town in the coal-mining region of southern Illinois could turn his fantasies into reality, anyone can. *You can!* You just have to treat your goal the way your dog handles a bone: Grab the dream, grip it tight and don't let anyone take it away from you.

I'm often asked, "Why don't you retire?
You've achieved the American dream. You
have enough money, a winter home in
Florida, a summer home in Michigan, an airplane, two boats and all the amenities you
need to make life comfortable. Why not quit
working so hard and *be happy with what
you've got?*"

Such a question misses the fundamental
truth about happiness: It doesn't come from
what we've got. It's generated by what we give.
One of my heroes, the late missionary doctor,
Albert Schweitzer, put it this way:

"You are happy, they say; therefore you are
called upon to give much."

It's because I *am* happy that I can't quit. The
happiness I enjoy doesn't depend upon what
I've achieved or acquired. It comes from what
I'm able to share.

Because not everyone understands this
great secret of happiness, I'm having a great
time spreading the word.

These days, instead of peddling gloom and
reporting human failure, as I did for so many
years on television, I've become a salesman
for success—*real* success. It's more fun showing people how great life *can be* than telling

them every night how rotten the world *is*.

So there's a selfish reason why I maintain such a demanding work schedule when I don't have to. Books, speeches, 520 broadcasts a year and running a business certainly is a load.

But to walk away now, to *lay back* and try to enjoy the fruits of previous labors, would bring no joy. I would lose the very machine that generates happiness. It is only in giving, sharing and helping others that personal happiness and true success are fully realized.

This kind of real success is available to anyone willing to work for it. When a soldier on bivouac during basic training asked his sergeant, "Where's my foxhole?" the sergeant replied, "Buddy, you're standing on it. Just throw the dirt out."

Most of us will find everything we need to reach our best and most worthy goals, right under our feet.

All we have to do is throw the dirt out.

So, if you want to be as terrific as your dog thinks you are, start digging!

Fourteen

As Big as You Think You Are

Size doesn't seem to matter as much to dogs
themselves as to the people who own them;
many small dogs have the pugnacious
attitude that would be downright dangerous
in a large dog.

—Dogs for Dummies

Things that upset a terrier may pass virtually
unnoticed by a Great Dane.

—Smiley Blanton

As I started to unload the fifty-pound bag of cat food from the van, Zachary, our grandson, volunteered to carry it into the house. Zachary was four.

I watched for a moment as he struggled to lift a bag that obviously was too heavy for someone his size. Finally, after a heroic but unsuccessful effort, he was ready for Grandpa's help and, between the two of us, we got the bag inside.

Sometimes we're too quick to tell a child, "You're not big enough." It's good for children and adults to *believe* in their capacities to perform *big jobs*.

Life will provide periodic reality checks to

163

keep us from dangerously overestimating what we can handle. Zach's firsthand experience with the fifty-pound bag was sufficient to put his ability into perspective. He didn't need a lecture from me telling him he was "too little."

For most of us, overestimating our abilities isn't the problem. The reality is, we think of ourselves as *smaller* than we are and our problems as *bigger* than they are.

This kind of thinking profoundly impacts the way we approach our problems and the outcome.

In an earlier chapter, I recounted how Bogey, a miniature dachshund, became number-one dog at our house despite the overwhelming size of Golum, a seventy-pound Doberman.

Bogey's leadership came not from his brawn but from his brain. Apparently, he'd never seen himself in a mirror. In his mind, he was just as big as Golum—maybe bigger. He walked with a swagger, head erect, tail high, taking no guff from man or beast. You could tell that Bogey thought of himself as superior to Golum in every way, including size and strength.

Dachsies are notorious for taking on dogs

many times their size. This rash courage, combined with their short legs and long bodies, made them ideal for the job they were originally bred to perform: finding, then overpowering badgers burrowed in underground tunnels. Often the vicious badgers were larger than the dogs sent in after them. Inevitably, the dachsies won because they never had any idea just how small they really were.

One of the worst mistakes we can make in life is to *over*estimate a problem and underestimate our ability to deal with it. Too many people worry that they'll be guilty of the reverse. They're always concerned that the problem is *bigger* and more terrible than they'd imagined, while their ability to deal with it probably is much less than they'd thought.

Study the biographies of people who've accomplished the most in any field and you discover that most of them believed they were bigger than they were. As a result, they eventually grew into the image they had of themselves.

The Wright Brothers were convinced their ideas about aviation were bigger than the formidable challenges of flight. Consequently, they were able, in the words of one historian, to "fly through the wall of impossibility."

Just *saying* we're big enough to face our challenges isn't the same as actually *believing* it. Talk is cheap.

A cowboy was about to leave the local saloon when he discovered someone had stolen his horse.

He stomped back into the place, flipped his gun into the air, caught it above his head without looking and fired a shot into the ceiling.

"Which of you sidewinders stole my hoss?" he demanded. Then he added, "If my hoss ain't back outside by the time I finish another drink, I'm gonna do what I done in Texas. And I sure don't want to do what I done in Texas."

Some of the locals shifted restlessly.

When the cowboy walked outside, his horse was back.

As he saddled up to ride out of town, one of the locals said, "Say, partner, just what was it you had to do in Texas that you didn't want to do again?"

And as he galloped away, the cowboy said, "I had to walk home."

Bluster and bravado are no substitutes for

honest belief in our ability to handle life's difficulties. Bogey was able to perform *like* a big dog because he honestly believed he *was*.

But how do we convince ourselves, honestly, that we really are up to a challenge? We do it by preparation and perseverance.

We become big enough first by imagining ourselves as capable, then by doing what's required to grow into the image.

James Earl Jones has one of the most distinctive voices in the world today. You've heard it in movies. You hear it daily announcing those familiar words, "This . . . is CNN." But this wonderful bass voice, which so eloquently combines velvety richness with distinct articulation, once belonged to a man who stuttered.

When James Earl Jones was a youngster, he stuttered so badly he had to use written notes just to communicate with teachers and with his friends. But in his mind, Jones was always bigger than his problem.

He knew that with determination and hard work, with training and perseverance, he could become as big in reality as he was in his imagination.

Consider some of the big people who might

have remained anonymous had they been willing to accept their challenges as being bigger than they were.

A newspaper once fired Walt Disney because they said he lacked ideas.

When Bob Dylan performed in his high school talent show, they booed him off the stage.

Fred Astaire, one of the greatest dancers ever to waltz out of Hollywood, received a stinging memo after his first screen test. It said: "Can't act. Slightly bald. Can dance a little." For as long as he was in show business, Fred Astaire kept that memo over the fireplace in his Beverly Hills home. The challenge it represented to him at the time was big, indeed. But Astaire knew he was bigger!

John Grisham is one of America's favorite authors. Like many avid readers, my wife, Renee has read everything he's written. But before he became such a popular novelist, Grisham had to overcome some very big problems:

His first novel, *A Time To Kill*, was turned down by twenty-eight publishers before he finally sold it.

Often someone will come up to me after

I've delivered a speech and ask, "Have you always been this confident in front of an audience?" Frequently, the questioner is a young person, eager to develop a similar kind of self-assurance.

No, I explain, I haven't always been at ease in front of an audience. In fact, as a teenager, I was quite shy—in some ways, introverted. But I did enjoy music and one day was invited to play a clarinet solo at a school variety show.

I wasn't exactly terrified, but I was nervous about going on stage. My aunt, who'd spent years as a vaudeville performer, gave me a couple of pointers which I've never forgotten.

She said, "First, before you go out there, figure out what's the worst that can happen to you. Once you face down your fear and realize that a poor performance won't ruin your life, then you won't be so anxious."

But the second thing she told me was even more important:

"The key to beating stage fright is to be prepared," she said. "Practice, practice, practice. Be sure that when you step out in front of that curtain, you're *ready*." Preparation is life's greatest confidence builder.

It was that simple two-step formula that

helped me then, and helps me now, to feel *big* enough to face even the largest, most sophisticated audience. We can only be as big as we think we are if we're prepared.

The next time you're facing some obstacle that you think is too big for you, consider this story about a game some scout troops used to play.

The scoutmaster would line up chairs in a pattern so that they created an obstacle course. Then, after studying the chairs, all the new scouts would be blindfolded and told to maneuver through them.

As soon as they had their blindfolds on, the older scouts would quietly remove all the chairs. One former scout who's now grown recalls how hilarious it was, watching those guys with the blindfolds on trying to weave their way through obstacles that weren't there.

Once we take off the blinders and look, realistically, at our problems, we often discover that some of *our* obstacles don't really exist. They were only in our minds. Or, if they do exist, they're not nearly so big and foreboding as we'd imagined.

When Glenn Cunningham was seven, he

was burned so badly in a school fire that doctors doubted he'd ever walk again.

But Glenn had been so motivated by his father to become a champion runner, walking was, for him, only a starting point.

At this juncture of his life, the dream seemed impossibly big and his chances of realizing it incredibly small. At least that's how it seemed to others. Not to Glenn. Despite intense pain, he did learn to walk. Then, he did just a little bit more. And a little bit more after that until, eventually, he was running again. Not fast, at first, but in time, fast enough to become the outstanding mile runner of his day.

Glenn Cunningham proved to be as big as he thought he was.

There is some risk in believing we're big enough to handle life, but the risk of not believing it is even greater. While there are no guarantees we'll succeed if we tackle life with confidence, it's absolutely certain we'll fail if we don't.

When a stranger spotted the backwoods farmer just sitting on the steps of his rundown shack, he asked the farmer, "How's your wheat coming along?"

"Didn't plant none," the farmer replied.

"Really? I thought this was good wheat country," the stranger said.

"Nope, I didn't plant," replied the farmer. "Was afraid it wouldn't rain."

"Well, what about your corn crop?"

"Nope, ain't got none. Afraid of corn blight."

"Then tell me," the stranger persisted, "What *did* you plant?"

"Nothin'," the farmer said. "I just played it safe."

And when *we* play it safe, when we accept the notion that we're *too little,* and the challenges *too big, nothing* is exactly what we'll get.

But don't take my word for it: Ask any miniature dachshund.

Fifteen

What's the Point?

If people were one-half as faithful to God and obedient to His commands as a dog is faithful to his master and obedient to his commands, we would have a far better world to live in than we yet have found.
—R. B. Harris

The purpose of life is a life of purpose.
—Robert Byrne

Have you ever wondered why God created dogs?

Probably not.

You may have questioned why he ever decided to make mosquitoes, ticks or rattlesnakes.

But not dogs.

Their purpose is obvious: They were put here to serve. They seem to recognize this and, for the most part, fulfill their purpose quite well.

Two skiers were marooned by a sudden snowstorm high up in the Alps.

Soon they spotted a Saint Bernard trotting toward them, the traditional keg of brandy hanging from her neck.

"Wonderful," one of the skiers shouted with delight. "Here comes man's best friend!"

"Yes," the other responded, "And look at the big furry dog that's carrying it."

Helping the lost and stranded is only one way dogs have earned their title—*best friend*.

Consider the countless ways they meet human needs: guiding the blind, herding sheep, locating lost children, hunting down criminals, sniffing out drugs, guarding homes and businesses—even promoting the recovery of ailing children and seniors.

Dogs have many talents but perhaps the most admirable is *dependability*. They're always there when you need them.

A human may not have time for us. A dog always will.

A human may deceive us, lie to us or betray us. A dog never will.

When Renee's sons, Jeff and Randy, were in grade school, they had a dachshund named JoJo. At bedtime, each boy enjoyed snuggling up with JoJo next to him. But, of course, the dog couldn't be two places at once.

Competition for JoJo became so fierce that, finally, Renee created a calendar showing where the dog was to sleep on any given night: Monday, Randy. Tuesday, Jeff. Wednesday, Randy, and so on.

Of course JoJo couldn't read. So what typically happened was this: If JoJo went to bed with Jeff, sometime during the night, she'd slip into the other room and hop up onto Randy's bed.

Renee recalls that almost every night, JoJo ended up dividing her time between the two boys. The dog seemed to know her job was to *serve* both. *Love* both. Bring *happiness* to both. JoJo didn't need a calendar to understand her purpose.

From the delight they provide children to the comfort they give seniors, it's apparent dogs instinctively know they were put on this planet for a reason.

From hunting birds to pulling sleds, from guarding houses to patrolling sheep, they've demonstrated a remarkable ability to be good workers as well as great friends.

Dogs derive obvious joy from helping us. Their work seems to bring them pleasure. Doesn't the fact that assisting us makes them so happy confirm that *service* is a primary purpose for their existence?

But the truth is, dogs don't have to *do*

anything to fulfill their purpose. Sometimes simply *being there* as a companion is a dog's highest calling.

Is the dog that calms a frightened child or comforts a lonely old person living out a lesser purpose than the one who sniffs out drugs or protects a business?

The interesting thing about purpose is, you can't contain it in a job description because purpose is different than work. It's much bigger. Much more important. Work is about *what* we do. Purpose is about *why we do it.* Dogs perform many kinds of jobs, and some perform no jobs at all. But they *all* have the same *purpose*: service.

So what about *us?* What's *our* purpose? Why were *we humans* put here? If we want to be as terrific as our dog thinks we are, maybe we should consider that question. Once we look at it carefully, we may discover that our purpose is the same as theirs.

When a Sunday School teacher told her class of third-graders that the reason we're all here is to serve others, one child raised her hand and said, "Well, I'd like to know what the *others* are here for!"

The idea that service to others is the

fundamental purpose of life is not new. It goes back at least to ancient Greek philosophy. It is at the heart of most major religions, including Christianity.

Jesus equated it to loving God: "As you do it unto others, you do it unto me." Even the great physicist, Albert Einstein, bought into the concept. One day, at the end of his lecture, he was asked by one of his students, "Dr. Einstein, why are we here?" It was a question that seemed more appropriate to the philosophy department than the science lab, but Einstein was ready.

To answer this fundamental question, he didn't need to resort to charts, graphs or sophisticated formulas. To Einstein, the answer was self-evident.

"Why, we are here," he said, "to serve others."

How could this scientist be so sure that service is our purpose? How could this brilliant thinker who'd spent a lifetime of professional skepticism, testing theories, demanding empirical evidence and questioning everything until it was proven—how could this genius declare so confidently that the purpose of life is to serve?

Einstein knew it the same way a dog knows:

because it feels right. Because it produces contentment and joy. Because it *works*. It's a self-evident truth like those the founders of our nation spoke about.

Service is our purpose because its value as a life principle can be tested.

When people in a family—or a community—adopt attitudes of serving each other, they're happier, healthier and more functional. Life runs more smoothly. When we make serving others our purpose, it's like putting on a suit that was tailor-made for us. It fits! Nobody has to explain that it's ours.

The reason this concept has survived as the basis of many philosophies and most religions is because it's proven itself in the laboratory of life. When we live selfishly, our mood turns sour. Relationships fall apart. Bitterness and cynicism replace happiness and contentment. Nothing functions as it should. Life is out of balance.

But when we live generously, when we see life as one big ongoing opportunity to help others, our days are vibrant. Relationships bloom. Renewed enthusiasm for life replaces resentment. Everything starts to work better. Life is in synch!

What we *do* in life makes a lot more sense once we understand why we're here in the first place. The answer to *that* question gives meaning to every other question. Until we discover a satisfactory answer, all the other answers don't add up to very much.

In this regard, dogs are lucky. They don't have to *think* about the question. We do. They're born with the answer built-in. We aren't.

A dog's purpose is immediately clear to everyone, including the dog. We, on the other hand, have to cut through the underbrush of life's ambiguities and blaze uncharted trails through all the confusion in order to *find* ours. Only then does it become *obvious*.

But, as anyone will tell you who has discovered *the secret*, it's well worth the search. One reason there's so much discontent and anxiety in our nation today—despite unprecedented prosperity—is because too many people have failed to confront life's paramount question: Why am I here? They've invested all their time and energy attempting to answer the "how-to's" of life without first answering the "what-for."

Of course, the "how" questions are important. How do I maintain my health? How do I perform better on the job? How can I improve

my relationships? How can I save enough
money for retirement?

Young people coming out of school have
their own list of important questions. What
career should I choose? Should I marry, and
if so, whom? Do I want children, and if so,
how many? Where do I want to live?

Such significant questions demand serious
answers.

But the answers to all these questions put
together won't add up to a happy, fulfilled life
if we fail to answer the *first* question, *What is
my purpose? What does it all mean? What's the
point?*

Rabbi Harold Kushner has written many
wonderful books, among them, *When All You
Ever Wanted Isn't Enough.*

For the person who's *never* dealt with life's
first question, there's never enough. Never
enough money. Enough power. Enough influ-
ence. Enough prestige. Enough sex. Enough
fun.

Until we know why we're here, life is a
treadmill that doesn't go anywhere. The
rewards we seek are always just out of reach.
Have you seen those dog races in cartoons
where a morsel of food is hung from a string

that dangles just beyond the dog's nose? The string is mounted to a stick which, in turn, is attached to the dog's harness. As the dog moves forward, the food does, too; always staying as far from the dog's mouth as when the race began. This device keeps the dog running by making him believe he'll eventually catch up to the food. He never does.

If we could find contentment in material comforts, if we could discover joy by answering all those other questions, we Americans would be deliriously happy, for never have people invested as much money and spent as much time attempting to find *those* answers.

The fact is, life will remain empty and unsatisfying until we've faced—and answered—the first question.

For many of us, the answer to life's basic question is found in our faith; we believe that existence is the result of a Creator, not of blind chance. It is embedded in our conviction that life *does* have a purpose and that our first job is to discover it.

Often people with no interest at all in religion discover such a faith as they struggle with *that question*. One such person was a scientist who thought all religion was a sham.

That prayer was a farce. Total humbug, in his view.

Then, one day, he became ill. This scientist lost not only his health, but his livelihood. His experiments were failing. He was nearly bankrupt.

Eventually, perhaps out of desperation, maybe simply out of boredom, this scientist made a pilgrimage to a shrine. He said to himself, "If I weren't an agnostic, I might experiment with this superstition. If this weren't such total folly, I might pray for something. Health, maybe. Or money?"

Suddenly, in spite of his skepticism, the man found himself crying out, "Oh, God, I beg you, enlighten my mind so that I may invent something very great to further human knowledge."

The scientist could hardly believe those words were coming out of his mouth.

But later he would write that, in some inexplicable way, he recognized in that moment his own *desire of desires*. He now understood something he could not prove.

And knowing, he went back to work with a new energy, a new attitude, a new *purpose*. The scientist was Galileo; eventually, his experiments produced the telescope.

To live without purpose is to be at loose ends, to muddle through life with no fixed point. No compass. No rudder. No way to accurately gauge whether we're doing it right. Imagine the chaos if all of us set our own watches and clocks wherever we felt like it. My watch might read 7:30 while yours showed 12:10. Life would be so confusing and nothing would get accomplished. Thankfully, the Naval Observatory near Washington maintains the exact time for all of us, precisely, by using special telescopes called photographic zenith tubes. This enables them to determine the exact time by measuring the relative positions of the sun and other celestial bodies.

A factory worker would stop each day in front of a jewelry store window, look at the big clock on display, and set his watch. One day the store owner happened to notice.

"I see you're setting your watch by my clock," he said.

"Yep. I do it every day. You see, I'm the watchman at the plant down the street and my job is to blow the five o'clock whistle. So, I have to know exactly what time it is."

The jewelry store owner was shocked.

"You can't do that," he said. "Don't you realize, I set my clock every day by your whistle?"

Purpose is the constant in our lives against which we "set" our priorities. It's not something we can create or make up. The true purpose of life can't be fabricated. It can only be discovered.

Every dog that ever rescued a stranded skier or protected a police officer or crawled into bed with a child or curled up in your lap knows that.

Sixteen

A Good Life

Often, we don't realize that we are grieving
not only for the pet we loved, but also for
the special time the animal represented.
                                        —*Dogs for Dummies*

To live in hearts we leave behind
            is not to die.
                                        —Thomas Campbell

Every book, like every life, must end.

It's been said, "We can never do *anything* for the last time without experiencing some sadness." So, as I sit here writing the final words for this book, I feel some melancholy.

Of course, it's not *all* sadness. There's also a sense of relief. Writing is hard work. It requires a disciplined routine and some self-sacrifice.

Completing this "project" brings with it the chance finally to relax. Tonight, instead of *writing* a book, I'll have time to *read* one.

But conclusions are sobering, even when we welcome them, because by their very nature they draw a permanent line between promise and performance.

The End means the door has been closed and what's done is done. What isn't done will never be done—at least not this time. Not on this project. Those words, *The End*, force us to ask, "Did I give it my best shot? With more effort, more thought, more commitment, more care, could I have produced something more worthy? Was I *capable* of more?"

As the author of several books, I've never arrived at the final chapter without confronting the same question I'm facing right now: Could it have been better? And the answer, always, is: of course. Absolutely it could have been better. I'm certain that artists, musicians, architects and others who create something from their imaginations inevitably ask themselves, toward *The End*, "Is this *really* what I intended? Does the work match the vision I had?"

No doubt when we reach the last chapter of our lives, we'll confront similar questions. Could I have lived better? Could I have been kinder? Could I have accomplished more with my life?

And no matter how good or kind or productive or successful we've been, the honest answer will have to be, "Of course I *could* have done better."

The best time to ask such questions is early on—at the beginning of a book or a life. That way we can reach *The End* with fewer doubts about our performance and whether we accomplished what we set out to do.

Renee and I have spent these past several days on Eleuthera, a charming island in the Bahamas that's provided a near perfect place for me to write and for her to read. Our mornings have begun, shortly after sunrise, with breakfast on the porch of the old house we're occupying. It's just up the hill from a spectacular inlet called Governor's Harbour and is surrounded by flowers and fruit trees.

The home belongs to J. J. and Mandy Duckworth, a young couple who raise orchids. But the most important thing they're growing is a two-year-old boy named John Lucas. Both the orchids—and John Lucas—obviously receive much tender love and care.

The Duckworths also have a dog, an aging hound they call Twiggy. He's of dubious heritage but J. J. tells me Twiggy has been a wonderful friend and companion for many years. Before J. J. and Mandy moved here from

Nassau, Twiggy was a watchdog, charged with guarding the family's business.

These days Twiggy would hardly be qualified to guard anything—even the small backyard papaya tree that provides us daily with fresh fruit. When she ambles into our yard and walks stiffly up our porch steps to greet us each morning, she looks about as threatening as the tiny lizards that scamper about the place.

Her gait is slow. Her back is nearly hairless in places because of an incurable fungus that's attached itself to her in her old age. The brown hair she has left is now speckled with gray. Twiggy can still see rather well, but her hearing is almost gone.

The old dog's not good for much these days except paying respects to visitors like us and providing some companionship to John Lucas. Mostly, she lies near the fence, soaking up the Bahamian sunshine. They say every dog has its day. Clearly, Twiggy's has long since passed.

The next time we visit this lovely island, I suspect Twiggy will be gone. She's writing her final chapter, if not the last paragraphs.

As sad as the farewell will be for the Duckworths, Twiggy's passing won't be tragic because Twiggy has lived a *good life*. She's fulfilled her purpose. She continues to enjoy the beauty in her surroundings and the people in her life.

Saying good-bye won't be easy because separation inevitably produces sadness. But *sad* isn't a synonym for *tragic*.

What's *tragic* is to never discover purpose. What's *tragic* is to never realize potential. What's *tragic* is to *waste life*.

When my father died at the age of sixty-six, I considered it, at the time, a *tragedy*. Here was a man on the threshold of retirement, with so many goals unreached, losing his battle with cancer. *His* father had lived into his nineties. For Dad to be cut down, so young, had to be a tragedy. What else could you call it?

There were so many things this vigorous and talented man had planned to do in the years ahead. He would paint pictures, compose music, write articles and even catch a few fish—activities he'd always enjoyed but rarely had time to pursue during his active years of ministry.

Time has taught me that Dad's life, even though it ended prematurely, did not end tragically because *he had found his purpose*. And, he'd found it early.

Dad figured out as a very young person that his primary purpose was to serve his God, and he'd done that throughout his life—by counseling, teaching, helping, inspiring, loving his family and consistently being *kind* to everyone he met.

How could the final paragraphs of such a person's life be labeled tragic?

Besides, Dad's certainty that life continues after death made *The End* for him merely a *transition*, not a *termination*. It marked the final chapter in one story and the introduction to a brand-new one.

The biggest tragedy is not that we die, but that we never fully live. We can't control how long our story will be. But we can control how *well* we *write* it.

When I began this book, I was uncertain how many chapters it should contain. Ten? A dozen? Twenty? Ultimately, the number didn't really matter. What mattered was the content. What would go into those chapters?

And so it is with our lives. The length of the work, the number of chapters we complete, isn't the most important. What counts is content.

Nicki was just past her fifty-fifth birthday when *The End* came for her. In one of our final conversations only a day or two before her death, she told me, "Mort, I'm really not afraid. And don't be too sad for me, because I've had a good life. I love you. I love our two wonderful children. I've been truly blessed. I don't want to leave all of you, but I'm ready."

Then she added three of the most profound words a dying person can utter:

"*Life* is good."

Nicki and I shared a belief in the afterlife, a certainty that God would not place within human beings a natural urge for which there was no possible fulfillment. For our thirst, there is water. For our hunger, there is food. For our ambitions, there are opportunities.

For our sex drives and need for companionship, we've been created male and female. It's clear a scratch has been provided for every itch.

Since the urge for *immortality* is the strongest craving of the human soul, it made no sense to us that *this* would be the one exception; the only void that could not be filled. Neither of us professed to have any idea, specifically, of what lay beyond the mysterious curtain of death.

The Bible, a centerpiece of our Christian faith, speaks in metaphor and allegory about the afterlife. To give a *literal* interpretation to its descriptions makes no sense. As much as I enjoy flying airplanes, I have no interest in sprouting wings. Anyone who's heard me play the accordion is praying that I'll never get my hands on a harp. Country roads and white-board fences are far more to my liking than gold-paved streets and pearly gates.

Nicki and I never spent much time trying to figure out the specifics of the afterlife. We were always too busy just trying to get the hang of this one. But we did both agree that whatever heaven is, it's more of a dimension of existence than a place. The childish con-cept of heaven as a locale "out there" or "up there" falters in the face of scientific under-standing of our physical universe.

No one has any inkling what this life will be like before we are born into it. I'm certain our rebirth into the next existence—whatever it is—will be just as full of wonderful surprises. So, while any attempt to fill in the details can never be more than interesting speculation, the concept of life's continuation was—for

Nicki and me—a matter of deep, personal faith. That life could—and would—continue in some other dimension seemed no more illogical to us than the incredible idea of life in the first place. Would it be *more* miraculous to *re*-create a life than to create it initially?

If a television receiver designed by a *human* mind can reassemble invisible waves that have been transmitted hundreds of miles and turn them back into a picture and sound, would reassembling a human personality be so difficult for the transcendent Mind who initially created it? Such faith, of course, is a matter of choice.

Just as a dog's purpose seems, to some of us, self-evident, so *human purpose* and *destiny* appear, to some of us, confirmed in the very structure and pattern of existence.

Gazing up at the stars, looking around at nature, peering down into our own hearts, we either recognize God's creative genius or we don't. Faith is not something we can be talked *into* or talked *out* of. That's why we call it *faith*. Like *purpose*, it isn't created. It's discovered.

And, like purpose, once we do discover it, we wonder how we ever missed it, how we ever got along without it.

Renee and I are at an age now where both of us have had to say good-bye to many friends and relatives in recent years. Parents, aunts, uncles, cousins and in-laws. The separations are always sad. We never like saying farewell to someone we love.

That includes our dogs. It may not be *tragic* to let go of a faithful pet that's lived a full and happy life of purpose. But it certainly is painful.

For years before Bogey and Golum reached *The End*, I recognized that telling them good-bye would be tough. It turned out to be even tougher than I'd imagined.

Bogey was first. That the aging dachshund's final chapter was being written could be seen increasingly in his failing energy. His waning appetite. His dimming eyesight and hearing loss.

The sound of an electric can opener no longer brought him bouncing into the kitchen. If it was time for his walk, only a loud hand clap could pierce his growing deafness.

Arthritis was taking a toll. One morning as I carried him to the back door of our condominium and gently sat him on the grass, he fell over. His stubby little legs no longer could support the body that had grown fat from inactivity. As he lay there on the dew-covered lawn, unable to get up, Bogey turned his head and looked at me with sadness in his eyes.

There no longer was enthusiasm or excitement in his face. His sparkling brown eyes once had been windows to Bogey's soul. On this particular morning, the windows were nearly closed. Cataracts had turned those once-mischievous eyes from bright brown to milky gray. When I tried to pick him up, he whimpered with pain. It was as though he were trying to tell me, "Please let me go. Don't make me suffer any longer." We'd reached the final paragraph. It was time for *The End*.

Tears rolled down my cheeks as I cradled Bogey in my arms, wrapped him in a towel, and began his final journey to the vet's office that he'd always hated so much. Renee went with me. Some things are just too hard to face alone.

As the vet prepared to end Bogey's suffering, I called Carey in California. After all, Bogey had been her dog. Would *always* be her dog. Carey had known for some time that *The End* was near for this little creature who'd comforted her—and her dad—through so much sadness. As I explained what was happening, I could hear Carey weeping softly at the other end of the line. But she concurred that what we were doing was right.

Bogey had always cried when we placed him on the vet's examining table. Always tried to get away. Not this time. Without a whimper, he lay there, accepting with gratitude the needle he'd always fought.

As we held his head and stroked it, Bogey slowly shut his eyes and found what he hadn't known for a long time: peaceful sleep, without pain.

For Golum, *The End* came only a few months later.

Not long after Renee and I married, Golum had left town to live with my son, Al. Giving Golum up was not easy for me; not after all we'd been through together. I also knew Golum was getting old and that *The End* couldn't be too far away.

But Al loved the dog as much as I did and, after all, Golum *was* his dog. The morning Al came for him, I took Golum out on our peninsula for one final run. His gray muzzle and slow walk told me this likely would be our last outing together.

A few months later, the phone rang. It was Al.

"Dad," he said with concern in his voice, "Golum's really not doing well. I think I need to bring him back to Detroit."

I knew exactly what Al meant. He didn't have to say it. He wanted to bring Golum "home" for the final chapter. During the time since he'd left us, the old fellow had gone down hill rapidly.

"His arthritis is much worse," Al said. "I don't think he can last much longer."

Once Al and Golum arrived at our house, it didn't take long to determine that *The End* was imminent. A consultation with the vet confirmed it. A date and time were set.

On Golum's last night, Al suggested that we buy him a hamburger. We'd always tried to feed our pets mostly pet food, believing this was better for them. But on this night, Golum got his hamburger. He devoured it, bun, lettuce, pickle and all.

It was a warm, summer evening. A cool breeze blew in off the lake. Al said he'd like to sleep on our porch. With Golum.

We brought out a small rollaway bed which we kept in a closet for extra company. Next to the bed, on the floor, we unrolled a sleeping bag. That would be Golum's bed.

Throughout the night, I found myself walking out to the porch to check on both of them. Each time I would find Al's arm hanging off the bed and around Golum's neck. Sometimes, he would be scratching the dog's ears or patting his head. It was clear Al wasn't sleeping much. Nor was I.

As the sun finally began to rise over the lake, I tried to find words to express what I'd been feeling during the long, sleepless night. Sometimes, words are easier to write than to speak. So while Al was dressing for the trip to the vet, I sat at my computer and wrote him a letter.

> Dear Al,
>
> The hardest part of love is letting go.
>
> Today, you and I are about to let go of Golum, and I know it's breaking both our hearts.
>
> You told me you didn't sleep much last night because of noise on the peninsula. I suspect it wasn't so much the noise outside as it was the sadness inside.

I've never felt quite so close to a pet as I do Golum. He and Bogey were there for us during your mom's illness. They were there to greet me at the door each night after we lost her.

If your mom were here now, she would offer reassurance about making the tough decision to let go when the time is right. She faced that. So did I.

The blackest moment of my entire life occurred the evening Dr. Burrows and I returned from taking Aunt Smiley back to Ohio.

As I walked into the house, your mom's nurse, Edie, met me at the door. There were tears in her eyes.

"Nicki doesn't want to fight any longer," she said. "And she really needs your permission to let go."

I was stunned. We knew her life was ebbing. But stop the fight? Give up? Let go?

Dr. Burrows took my shoulders. Tears welled up in his eyes. Al, you know he was much more than our doctor. He was our close friend.

"Mort, it will be the most difficult thing you've ever had to do. But it will be the most compassionate thing for Nicki."

I stumbled up the stairs, choking back my own tears and took a seat on the edge of your mom's bed. She was awake. Her eyes looked so tired. She was pale. The fight had been long and difficult.

"Honey, I don't want to continue," she said. "I just want to stop taking medication and let go."

Nicki knew—I knew—that without pills and shots, her system would begin to quickly shut down.

Her heart, her kidneys, her lungs— everything would just quit.

Al, I know about letting go. Yes, we could have extended her life for another few days, perhaps. But was it life?

No, we wouldn't have lengthened her life. Had we ignored her desperate plea to let go, we would have extended her death and prolonged her suffering.

Your mom had lived a good life. She

knew she was deeply loved. It was time.

Dogs can't make that choice. They are at our mercy.

I know the days ahead won't be easy for you, nor for me.

I know I'll cry when we have to say a final good-bye to this big old hunk of a dog. I'm choking up now just thinking about it.

Al, there's little I can say or do to ease what we feel this morning.

Today, it comes down to raw emotion.

To feelings.

To memories.

To love. And loss.

I love Golum, too, Al.

And I love you.

As it had been for Bogey, Golum's transition was peaceful. He whimpered, but did not wince, as the needle was inserted. I stroked his back. Al cradled his head. There was a final look of recognition, then the eyes closed and he was gone.

Al asked the vet if he could spend a few

minutes alone with his dog. I waited in the reception area.

They say that when a person is drowning, their entire life flashes before them. I don't know if it's true.

I do know that in the few minutes Al spent with our beloved friend, a *dog's* lifetime played itself out for me.

Not since his mother's death had I seen my son hurting with such intensity. We drove home without speaking, each of us dealing privately with our grief. As we pulled into the driveway, I noticed that Al was holding Golum's collar and tags in his hand.

"I thought I'd like to keep these," he said.

•   •   •

So how do I conclude this book? What do I say, finally, about trying to be as terrific as my dogs thought I was?

Only that it's a tall order. I may never achieve it. But I'll tell you this: I'll *never* be as terrific as I *know* they were.

And one more thing. I keep wondering whether these two buddies of mine have made it to heaven. Is there an afterlife for dogs?

Who can say? I suppose that will remain one of life's many unsolved mysteries.

But I *do* believe that God created those two guys. I do believe he gave them the most wonderful gift any creature can have: *purpose.*

That must mean he loved them, too.

And if he loved them as much as I did, it only figures that he would want to see them again.

THE END?

About the Author

Mort Crim was a broadcast journalist for over thirty-five years, working as a correspondent with ABC, New York and as a senior editor and anchor for WDIV-TV, Detroit. Currently, he is host of the award-winning radio feature, *Second Thoughts*, heard on more than 1,200 stations nationwide. His previous books include *Second Thoughts: One Hundred Upbeat Messages for Beat-Up Americans* and *Good News for a Change*.

Visit his Web site at: *www.mortcrim.com.*

More Thoughts from Mort Crim

1999 Audie Award Winner!

Second Thoughts

One Hundred Upbeat Messages for Beat-Up Americans

> "Mort's essays are like the voice of an old friend: kind, steady encouraging—and available at 4:00 A.M. when the world looks bleak. Gentle wisdom from an instant ally."
> —Diane Sawyer
> ABC-TV

SECOND THOUGHTS

One Hundred Upbeat Messages for Beat-Up Americans

Mort Crim
television anchor, radio broadcaster and creator of the internationally syndicated series *Second Thoughts*
Foreword by Jeff Daniels

Code # 5661 • Quality Paperback • $12.95
Code #570X • Two 90 minute audiocassettes • $14.95

A collection of 100 essays reflecting celebrated broadcaster Mort Crim's conclusions about life after 35 years of covering world events, *Second Thoughts* is about solutions, triumphs and faith. Within these pages you will find security and inspiration and realize that each one of us makes a difference in the world.